THE
MOTHER
LOAD

When Your Life's on Spin Cycle

THE MOTHER LOAD

and You Just Can't Get the Lid Up!

Caryl Kristensen *and* Marilyn Kentz
The Mommies

Cliff Street Books
An Imprint of HarperCollins*Publishers*

HarperCollins books may be purchased for educational, business, or sales promotional use. For information please write: Special Markets Department, HarperCollins Publishers, Inc., 10 East 53rd Street, New York, NY 10022.

FIRST EDITION

Designed by Elliott Beard

ISBN 0-06-019180-5

98 99 00 01 02 ❖/RRD 10 9 8 7 6 5 4 3 2 1

The Motherload is dedicated to our families: Richard, Marcy, Aaron, Richie and Pfilipa, and Len, Bryce and Eric, who have been generous in allowing us to share stories of their lives in the hope that other families know that laughing at ourselves is the key to loving each other; and our own mommies, Lina and Claire, who still love us even when we are bad.

And to the memory of Erma Bombeck, the queen of mommy humor, who continues to pave the way and inspire us.

Contents

Acknowledgments

We would like to gratefully acknowledge all the people who have helped us along the way; people who have been there and stayed there, giving us encouragement and support through all our various incarnations:

Mary McCutcheon, Billy Cohen, Judy Pastore, Robin "Otto" Tate, Mark Victor Hansen, Jack Canfield, Mike August, Viki Vyinello, Mallory Matulich, Marilyn Forrest, Tom and Lilka Areton, Lynn Lott, Jim Shreiber, Betty Fanning, Tim O'Donnell, Brian Peck, Jimmy Jam Campbell, Michele Conklin, Perry Simon, Kathy Tucci, Gail Josephs, Gary Hart, Kerry McCluggage, Stewart Kraznow, Nancy Alspaugh, Lisa Kridos, Alan David, Mark Teitelbaum, Leslie Garson, Dan Strone, Diane Reverand and especially the old Petaluma neighborhood.

Introduction

When another parent tells you about a problem she's having with her child, what's the first thing that comes to your mind? Is it, "Oh, that's too bad. I'm so sorry. Maybe I can help"? Well, we think that would probably be your *second* response. If you're anything like us, you're first thought is, "Thank God it wasn't my kid!"

We're "The Mommies," and like most mommies, we believe it's our job to make you feel better about yourselves. And since we're too busy to nurse each one of you personally, we wrote a book.

Nobody's perfect. No one. We're just normal, slightly flawed human beings trying hard to keep a balance and not send too many children to the therapist. And we need each other to validate that we're doing okay.

What if we only had the people in the news to compa
ourselves with? Of course we'd be very grateful that it wasr
our husband that was going around with a really bad toupe
biting everyone, but what makes it into the evening new
doesn't really speak to our everyday lives. Compared to th
average soap star, we're sexless and way too fat. And you cer
tainly can't use those TV talk show participants as any kin
of measurement. These people are the unwashed masses
One look at them and you're *really* thanking God that it's nor
your kid.

Magazine articles tell us how we and our children *should*
behave, how often we should be having sex and how everything in our house causes cancer. While the articles can be
good for suggestions and entertainment, what we need most is
to know we're not alone.

After returning home from a family vacation, don't you feel
better when your girlfriend admits that she gained ten pounds,
too? Isn't it a relief when she says she also found her husband's
driving to be extremely annoying and that every time she tried
to tell a story, her ten-year-old also interrupted with, "No, it
didn't happen like that"?

These days we don't have the opportunity to learn from the
wise quilter working on the patch next to us that our thoughts
and feelings and kids and husbands are normal. There's no
time for morning coffee with an intimate neighbor unless it's
with Matt, Katie and Al. So we try to connect with others while
distributing oranges to energetic soccer players or waiting for
our daughter's braces to be tightened.

We'd like to invite you to visit our world. A typical world
where mistakes are made and laughed about. Where the only
thing that's perfect exists in our imagination. You'll wipe your

row and say, "Whew, I'm glad I'm not the only one who
inks like that!"

So, make yourself a nice cup of tea, put down the laundry,
give yourself a little well-deserved break, read a chapter or two
and come laugh with us. You are not alone.

Caryl & Marilyn

Big Mac, Prozac, Living on the Cul-de-Sac

Caryl

Just as with our mothers before us, the "Suburban Code" is well in place. It is ever-changing and ever-evolving. The sooner you crack the code, the less likely it is that you will become its victim. Now, if you live in the city and are thinking, "That's not me!" think again, because suburbia can also be a state of mind. If you have even once lingered on a minivan ad and then checked to see if it had good drink holders, you are there.

The burbs, like every subculture, has its own set of unwritten rules. You must know that if you pull into suburbia and unknowingly veer off in the wrong direction, there are certain red flags that will make you a marked person. There is a group mentality as strong as the Teamsters in suburbia, so it's best to just play along. For example, if you are a woman and show up in anything overly sexy or provocative, you are going to be

labeled "Bitch Meat" by your neighbors. If you wear a tube t[
to the nipple line of your size D chest, like one sorry wom[
we drove out, the other women will gang up on you. Here's th[
biggest cul-de-sac rule ... there will be no tempting of th[
well-trained "sex-once-a-month" husbands.

The uniform is simple, a T-shirt and jeans or sweats. O[
days like teacher conferences, you may upgrade with a blaze[
(Consult Target if you are confused.) If you paint you[
dwelling a color other than the preaccepted muted earth tone[
that surround you, expect to be mocked. And never, ever[
under any circumstances, leave your children home alone and[
unattended with your husband during football season.

In the burbs we travel like packs of dogs. The dominant
females lead the social calendar, Tupperware parties and decorating trends. The females also determine the mating season.
The males coach the puppies' teams, hang Christmas decorations and burn the meat. All other pack members look
out for one another's babies, helping to shuttle them back
and forth and parenting in absentia. We live, die and decorate
by the code. For those of us in the never-ending quest for a
"Cleaver"-esque existence, this is a way of life ... this is medi-
ocrity at its best. Welcome to our world.

Did you imagine, when you were young and idealistic, a
detailed picture of how your life would turn out? And then
when you got to that time, not a single thing resembled your
fantasy? Well, my first years in the suburbs were just that for
me. I was an artist. I had a degree in graphic design. I was supposed to be living in San Francisco on Union Street among the
galleries and cafes, talking about art and working for Primo
Angeli, the famous designer. My reality, on the other hand, was
Petaluma, a farm town north of San Francisco. I drove a minivan, lived in a cul-de-sac and had a baby sucking on my breast.

was torn between being deeply in love with my son and choosing to live like a bohemian artist. I hadn't planned on getting pregnant so soon, but as one of eleven children myself, it's not as if I wasn't aware of my very dominant egg supply. Then I married that cute Dane, with sperm from the lineage of Vikings that ruled the oceans in those big ugly boats. It was stronger than the two of us. We had a baby and we moved to Petaluma because it was affordable and because we wanted our son to have what we had growing up.

So there I was smack in the middle of the "sac." I was isolated, without a car and knowing no one, as my husband went off to work every day with real people. What do people here do all day? Well, it wasn't long before that question was answered. Within the first month of moving in, I received so many invitations from women I had never met, to a whole slew of evening parties/"get-togethers." There was Tupperware and Mary Kay and crystal sales and home decorating and photo album making and Bunko and on and on . . . My curiosity got the best of me. I attended each one the first time around with enthusiasm. It was great meeting so many people like myself. I was also happy to find out that these get-togethers were just a flimsy excuse for us to get together and drink.

There was, however, one interesting invitation I received, one with some substance. One of my neighbors was going to run a book study out of her home on *Children: The Challenge,* a parenting book by Rudolf Dreikurs. Well, Bryce was four months old and I was certainly feeling challenged. I looked forward to going to at least one pseudo-intellectual neighborhood gathering.

Marilyn

One might wonder how my counterculture, liberal self fit into the suburbs. Before you get too judgmental, though, I just want to say for the record that by the time I had children I was no longer protesting or chaining myself to any building. Please note that I didn't name any of my newborns after a flower, a mountain, a state, a season, a goddess or a slang word. The last time I smoked pot I was twenty-six. My son Aaron was a little baby springing in the doorway all snuggled into one of those boingy jumpers that clamp to the door frame, laughing wildly. Aaron was born to bounce. And for those of you, our President included, who are unfamiliar with getting stoned, things become brighter, more in focus, intensified. I took one unforgettable look at that drooling, leaping, laughing, swinging little sticky-faced thing bouncing in my doorway and said, "What is it?" Then I prayed, "Please get me through this." But I think God mistook my prayer to mean: Please get me through this particular moment. No more mind-altering devices. I knew I was going to need all my faculties for this child. I stopped hitchhiking, tie-dying and astral flying. I threw away my halter top and headband, got me a pair of shoulder pads and a blazer jacket, stopped saying "far out," traded in my Volkswagen Bug for a minivan and headed for suburbia.

As a matter of fact, the change didn't really hit me until the summer of '82, when I was sitting out on my front porch one hot evening in my Kmart lawn chair beside a couple of friendly neighbors, each of us sporting a martini in our hands. The van was parked in my freshly cleansed driveway while my kids jetted past me on their Big Wheels. We were eating this new bean dip recipe out of my Tupperware bowl with tortilla chips in its "Modular Mate," and I believe I was complaining about taxes when I stopped in midsentence. That diminishing little grain of anti-establishment left in my soul made me freeze right there on the front porch. Beads of sweat started forming on my forehead. As if in slow motion, I took a good hard look around me and then ran back into the house, lit some incense and meditated for about twenty minutes. Ah, the burbs.

Caryl

*O*ne evening I attended the "Progressive Party" that had been organized by an especially enthusiastic "sac" member. This was the night that I first met Marilyn. She looked exactly like Karen Valentine. I was forced to go into instant *Room 222* dialogue. "Mr. Dixon . . . Oh, Mr. Dixon . . ." She laughed at that and I liked her. I must tell you, by this time she had totally transformed herself from that hippie she described. She met all the "sac" criteria. Nuclear family, middle management, clean-cut hubby and . . . she was wearing pumps. Yes, Marilyn . . . you were too wearing pumps.

As it turned out, it was Marilyn who had sent the pseudo-intellectual invitation, and it was she who would be running the book study. I also caught her snickering at the hideous all-gray paint job of the home we were in for hors d'oeuvres. She

told me she liked me because of my artistic handwriting on th
RSVP I made to her invitation. I knew in two seconds of sha
lowness that this was yet another artist trying to turn her cul
de-sac into Union Street. Our friendship was born.

If I ever got out of the house, I knew it would be with thi
woman. My depression began to lift. Marilyn and I would
meet in the middle of the street and chat about everything
but mostly we would chat about the other neighbors. It
became the time of day I looked forward to the most. I was
beginning to forget about Union Street. In fact, it had been a
month since I had even set foot in San Francisco.

*T*he part I love most about living on a cul-de-sac is the pre-
tense that we're giving our kids the wholesomeness we
had growing up. Safe within the sac, it becomes "my old neighborhood." I loved the warm and familiar feelings I had when I
folded clothes in my living room with the front door wide
open, listening to the music of the children playing hide-and-
seek. If I should hear tears over a skinned elbow, I'd run outside
only to find two other mothers already taking care of it.

My favorite time of day was late afternoon. I'd check down
the street to see if *they* were out there yet. Around three-thirty
all the moms in the 'hood would gather on someone's lawn for
about an hour while the kids rode bikes and played in front of
us. That's the place where we'd get our therapy. Whether it

was just to complain about a dorky husband, a naughty child, a judgmental mother, an inconsiderate teacher, a bad haircut, an imaginary lump or a roll into the wet spot, this was our support system. It was the time of day when I learned I'm not alone and that we all share the same fear that *our* kid will be the one to grow up and become a criminal.

We'd sit out there with our Lillian Vernon catalogs and order Christmas stuff, then someone, usually Joanne, would have us cracking up over something hideous she'd done the night before. Like the time she called a wrong number. She was lying down one evening with a headache and wanted her sixteen-year-old son, Brian, to bring her some Advil. So, instead of calling out his name from ten feet away, she dialed his private number in his room. She must have dialed incorrectly, because she got a wrong number. Though she assured us that her regular response is to apologize, this particular time she panicked and hung up.

The phone rang right away. More panic. She thought, "Oh no! They have star-six-nine!" Then, "Oh, it's probably just a coincidence," but just in case, Joanne disguised her voice. We pointed out that she had not yet used her regular voice, but Joanne said that she didn't want to take any chances.

In a deepened tone Joanne answered, "Hello?" An irate voice barked, "Who is this?" She panicked and hung up again. The phone began to ring immediately, so she ran to the kitchen to turn off the answering machine, but didn't get there in time. "Hi, you've reached seven-six-two—" Joanne pulled the answering machine out of the wall. Ed, her husband, came in only to find Joanne standing in front of the ringing kitchen phone, clutching the bedroom phone and answering machine, one arm stretched out in the "stop" position. With terror in her eyes, she spit out, "Don't touch it!"

RING. RING. RING. Ed, seeing a madwoman, was completely bewildered. *RING. RING.* Curious kids came out from their bedrooms. *RING. RING.* "DON'T *ANYBODY* TOUCH THE PHONE! DO YOU HEAR ME?" Brian and Jamie just stared at their mother.

She finally turned off the ringer, but the phone in the garage wouldn't shut off. Her family stood frozen, eyes glued to the crazy woman, afraid to ask questions.

Realizing that this star-69 lady was relentless, Joanne asked Brian to call her from his private number to undo the star connection with the family phone. He dialed with great hesitancy. The star-69 lady answered and Brian asked for someone, anyone. She started yelling at Brian.

Meanwhile, Joanne was pacing in the background barking, "Admit it, Brian. Admit you made a mistake. Now tell the lady you're sorry and get off the phone." Tales from the 'hood. Pure afternoon delight.

Caryl

By the fifth Tupperware invitation, I had grown weary. Not only had I memorized the dealer's whole speech, but I could recite it backward and forward. I could also do it with an accent or in a mocking tone or as an old woman. I think I made the last dealer cry and quit. I must have kept her from winning that minivan. I didn't mean to, it's just that after a while in the suburbs, you have to find ways to inject life into

ed subjects. Besides, I was getting my first taste of perform-
. I loved to entertain the women, even if it was at someone
e's expense.

"Bunko" tore through the suburbs like a wild fire. For those
you urbanites who have never had the pleasure, let me
plain. It's a really simple dice game that you would pay three
cks to play. At the end, the winner took home a new wooden
w or something. This game is good because you change tables
d partners a lot and it requires no brain, so you can concen-
ate mostly on the gossip. The rotating of the players enables
ou to cover all the information from the entire neighbor-

Paul and Len admire their fabulous fruit skewers as the meat burns behind them!

hood in under two hours. You gotta hand it to us . . . we are efficient.

My other favorite cul-de-sac friend, Judy, and her husband Paul, became our link to sanity. Judy had two kids under the age of two and she was looking for an outlet as often as I was. When she got home from work she would fill the little blow-up pool in the backyard with water. Then she'd call me and say "Surf's up." I'd gather my Coke and chips, and Bryce, too, and I would go poolside until the sun went down. None of us had any money—we spent it all on the mortgage—so often we would share our food to create one big dinner. "I have some chicken." "Well, I have some broccoli." "Good, bring it over, we'll call it dinner!" It began to feel like living in a tribe. In a way, Marilyn had a second commune up and running.

I think our husbands were jealous of our intense organizational skills. We all began settling in and creating this huge nest. The dreaded life of a parental unit ended up being some of the best times of my life. I actually began to look forward to things like Target grand openings and sidewalk sales and cul-de-sac block parties. We'd share decorating tips and sponging techniques. I was into the whole country motif there for a while, until my husband put his foot down and said, "Honey . . . no more wooden ducks." (I missed the whole Southwestern trend . . . I must have been breast-feeding.) Sometimes the entire neighborhood would come down with the same "decorating virus." One day you had blank front doors, the next day they all had dried-flower wreaths nailed to them.

Saturdays in the cul-de-sac were especially fun. All the kids would be out on their Big Wheels and bikes and the husbands mowing lawns with babies in backpacks . . . well, except for Richard, Marilyn's husband, "Mr. Safety." He would mow with ear coverings to muffle the sound, clear plastic goggles for his

es, and big leather boots just in case a blade of grass might
up and cut his leg open. It was a Saturday ritual to watch
chard suit up and prepare to mow. I knew that every holi-
y our friend Renee would display incredible control of her
mily by getting them to dress monochromatically. She used
deny it until one day I caught her red-handed pulling out of
er driveway with the entire family in red bandanas and denim
n their way to a western party. I knew in the winter I could
ount on Paul chopping wood on his driveway while the other
eighbors helped stack it and then stole a few logs for them-
elves. I began to treasure our suburban customs.

Marilyn

It's been a tradition in our little Petaluma neighborhood that
when one us would leave for the maternity hospital, the rest would wait two
days, then gather
together and deco-
rate the front of the
house with crêpe
paper, IT'S A BOY / GIRL
lettering and balloons.
We'd all be there wait-
ing in the driveway for
that first preview of the
teeny new addition.

Welcoming another member into the sac.

It's been a long time since we've done that, though. I belie
we've all either tied off, cut our husbands off or turned off. T
balloons these days are more often black and say HAPI
FORTIETH. Young families are moving to newer neighbo
hoods, our kids are getting acne and their driver's license
we're repainting the outside of the house again and the cycl
continues. I have become my mother.

Sometimes there's competition on the sac. Christmas ca
bring out a sense of warfare in some folks. Now I ask you
how simple can a person's life be if the supreme goal is to
have more lights, wooden candy canes, reindeer, toy soldiers
nutcrackers, mice and little elves than anyone else in the ter
ritory? Hearts can be broken when the judges disallow a live
animal motif. One neighbor put his back out with a little slip
on the roof. Another caused a major power outage.
Suspicions of sabotage float around the 'hood. I've
always wanted to gather a group of therapists, dress
them up like Dickens's carolers and unleash them on the
unsuspecting zealots.

Mostly we were there to help each other. When our friend
Chrissy was pushing forty and not yet pregnant, we all gathered around her, eager to help, turkey baster in hand. One early
morning I came by for a cup of coffee and she was on the
phone with an open ovulation kit in her hand. She was in her
white bathrobe describing to the twenty-four-hour hotline
nurse the exact shade of pink the little circle was showing. I
noticed that she could only convey it through decorating
terms, a woman after my own heart. "No, no. It's more melon
than mauve, with a touch of coral."

She hung up and reported, "The nurse said I'm either just
starting to ovulate or just finishing. Keith's still home. Should I

?" Meanwhile Caryl walked in, Chrissy laid it all out for her d together we all agreed she should try.

As she entered the bedroom, we heard Keith say, "Oh, oh . . . e's got her lab coat on." Caryl poured herself a cup of coffee d about ten minutes later Chrissy was back in her .throbe/lab coat joining us in the kitchen for a morning cup. aryl and I yelled out, "Keith! You animal, you!"

We taught Chrissy the theory of putting your bottom in the r to use gravity to encourage the sperm to swim in the right irection. By the time Keith was dressed and ready for work, he iscovered his wife in an intriguing position on the kitchen oor. Caryl and I got up from our kitchen stools and began a ertility dance around her. He immediately exited.

This kind of intimacy is prevalent in women anyway and is even stronger in the sac.

When we first moved to L.A., I was so surprised to find the same type of existence here that we had left behind in Petaluma. I expected to find nothing but violence, cement, bad traffic and aggressive, irritated, phony people. Sure, those things are a constant in L.A., but there are also tree-lined streets, fancied-up mailboxes, kids playing in and out of each other's homes, neighbors helping other neighbors and unbelievable creativity. Unfortunately, all those negative parts of the big city now exist in Petaluma as well.

My new neighbors seem to know the "Rules of the Sac." All the houses around here are of subtle earth tones and the only sorry old tube tops I see around L.A. are hanging out on Sunset Boulevard looking for Hugh Grant.

And as far as my resistance to becoming part of the establishment is concerned, I realized, as I was putting some granola in my shopping cart and the soft Muzak playing gently over the

speakers was The Ray Conniff Singers exuding, "You are t
Walrus. I am the walrus. Goo goo ga joob," that we're all he
The "hip" are in the 'hood! Let's hear it for our Weber-lov
neighbors! The Revolution is alive and well and living in t
cul-de-sac! Goo goo ga joob.

We're Always Right, Face It!

I Do,
I Don't,
I Do

*W*edding ceremonies are sweet, don't you think? It's our link with tradition; sometimes it's the bride and groom's only link. I wonder what percentage of guests with sentimental tears on their cheeks and smiles on their faces are really thinking, "I give it a year." I'm sure it was over 50 percent at my first wedding. It was probably even more at my second.

The week after my fifteenth wedding anniversary with Richard, his ex-wife called, and as soon as I got off the phone I childishly started humming, "Nanny, nanny, nanny ... I've been married to him longer than you ever were. Ha-ha-ha-ha-ha-ha." It was at that pathetic moment that I realized that my anniversary had been the past weekend and neither Richard nor I had remembered. I stood there a little stunned, started giggle and thought, "How could *I*, Miss Poignant, forget such an important anniversary? Our crystal anniversary. How embarrassing."

When I tried to remember what we ended up doing on that date, I was surprised. You see, Marcy had spent the weekend with a friend and we ended up going out for a movie and romantic dinner. The next morning I was actually in the mood for sex. We made love and then spent the day together holding hands and flirting with each other while looking for antiques at the flea market. It was all the things we would have planned to do if we had remembered without it being contrived. I was touched and was sure this *proved* that it was *true love*. It's a good thing that our anniversary hadn't fallen on the weekend before, when he was really bugging me.

M Richard and I got married eighteen years ago on a boat. The boat was in our backyard. Our closest friends stood on the terrace and down the stone steps that led to the unfinished sloop, which was cradled in a wooden structure on our back lawn. The guests witnessed our ceremony in their finest nautical attire. It touched my heart to see my eighty-nine-year-old Italian grandmother in a cute little red, white and blue cotton sailor dress standing next to a family of whales. I wondered if it brought back memories of her trip to Ellis Island. The minister looked like an eighteenth-century captain, Hook with both hands. Our combined kids, who were five, six and nine years old at the time, were on board with us, their sailor suits already dirty. Richard made an extremely handsome groom in a military kind of way, though the sweet tears glistening on his cheeks as he tried to speak his vows did not fit the demeanor of an admiral.

I was a little nervous. Would it be different this time? Would be *true love* this time? The wedding ceremony certainly was different. It was a far cry from the white gown and tuxedos racing Saint Eugene's Cathedral fourteen years earlier, when arry and I had said "I do." Some of the guests were the same. The food was different. The band was different. The groom was different. I know I was different. At eighteen, the color of my bridesmaids' dresses seemed much more important to me than whether or not our love would last.

We all looked so cute with our hair teased up all the way to heaven. My white lipstick matched perfectly with my white Empire-waist wedding gown. I had no doubts about getting married that first time around. Everything was color-coordinated. It was a good omen. I believed it was a marriage made in high school heaven and that I would be happy for the rest of my life. Hey, I had watched a lot of Disney.

Larry and I were such young pups back then. We were fresh out of high school. The year was 1966. Looking back, I can't say we were experiencing *true love*, though at the time I believed we were. The truth was that we both really wanted to get out of the house. When we made the decision to get married, not one of our parents even thought to recommend holding off for a while. I think the need for parent-child separation might have been mutual. Or perhaps it was just a sign of the times. In 1966 the social standards dictated that it was better to enter the sacred union of marriage, even if you were a teenager, than to participate in unsanctified sex. So, with our parents' hearty approval, I began my first adventure as a teenage wife on April 15, the day taxes are due.

Our marriage lasted for twelve years. Together we experienced army life in Oklahoma during the Vietnam War, groovy vegetarian counterculture life running naked among

the redwood trees, and a hip life in the world of music, whe
Larry was a bass player for a group called Bob Ward and th
Cigar Band and I was a tap-dancing Havana. Then in 1974 w
enriched our lives by becoming the parents of baby Aaron.
wasn't a bad marriage at all. We helped each other grow up.

Many years had passed since Larry and I were "The Coc
Couple" of Montgomery High. We were both very enamore
with toddler Aaron, but not at all with each other. It was as i
we were always tired when we were together.

When Larry and I were thirty, I met Richard. He was writing a book and I was an illustrator. I think I fell in love with
Richard the moment I met him. I was committed to my marriage to Larry, though, so I ignored my feelings as best I could.

Through the years Larry and I would take turns protecting
and being caretakers of each other. Okay, maybe he took care
of me a little more often. We leaned on each other until
we no longer needed to lean. Then, when the time came
to break up, I didn't know how to do it, so instead I slept
a lot. The marriage was tired. I wish I could say that it was horrible, threatening and abusive, just in case Dr. Laura ever reads
this, but the truth is, it was only tired.

After a few months of working together on Richard's book,
we began having an affair. So much for my commitment to
marriage. I let myself fall in love. I was passionately in love
with Richard. I still am.

I felt guilty and wanton and crazy. I couldn't sleep or eat or
think straight. I was not of this world. I couldn't bear the insanity. So I took the easy way out. The selfish way out. No, I didn't
lie and try to hide it. I didn't ask for a divorce or separation. I
was much too chicken for that. I simply told Larry about it. I
purged. I got it all off my chest and then I pretty much asked
his permission. Surprisingly, he gave it. I said that I was sleep-

; with Richard and I didn't much like his choice in mattresses, would he please help me move the mattress from our spare om to Richard's? (Well, Larry had a big pickup truck!)

Larry was a firefighter and had a schedule where he slept at e firehouse every other night. I took up that same schedule ith Richard. One morning on his way to the fire station, arry kissed me good-bye, loaded the spare mattress into his uck and dropped it off at Richard's. He seemed to be taking rather well.

I understand how you might be judging me right now. I on't blame you. It was the seventies. I assure you I was not an nomaly. It was a sign of the times. Free Love had not yet died ut in California. I'm glad it since has.

I had been struggling over the situation for nearly a year. Should I stay with my dear high school friend, the father of my son? Or should I go to the man I truly loved? Both Larry and Richard were tolerant of my bed-hopping. Larry told me numerous times that he understood, and never once did he beg me to stay. I don't think he even mentioned it casually. I had seen enough movies to know that a person begs his *true love* to stay, not delivers a more comfortable mattress for them.

Now, twenty years later, I understand what happened and I'm compelled to forgive myself. After all, Larry was my boyfriend in high school. How many mothers today would encourage their child in his or her senior year to plan both a high school graduation party and a wedding a few months later? It's ridiculous. All the guests would be the same, for God's sake.

I wonder if maybe Larry was waiting for a breakup to happen because one morning, after having a dream where we said good-bye in the kindest fashion, I woke up, turned to him and asked, "Have you ever thought about separating?"

He responded, "Yeah." Did I hear a touch of excitement his voice? Then he asked, "Have *you*?"

I tentatively responded, "Yeah."

"Then let's do it!" He seemed ecstatic.

"Okay!" I was excited.

We then proceeded to make love for the last time; he helped me pack my bags and waved good-bye from the front porch. could be wrong, but I thought I saw him wipe his brow an exhale a sigh of relief as he went back into the house. The nex day he delivered a huge laundry basket of my dirty clothes to Richard's.

As simple and lighthearted as it sounds, that's just how easy it was. I'm not saying that the separation and divorce that followed were without sentiment or emotional moments. I was very shaken up. I was saying good-bye to a dear friend, a person with whom I had shared a life and, most important, a child. Some of the difficulty came from the fact that there was no one to curse or blame. In a strange way, it's easier to break up if you despise the person. In the end I know it was my fault and yet I don't regret it. The separation, like the relationship, just kind of trailed off.

One day I stopped by my old house to pick up some mail and Larry was at work. I noticed that he had leftover barbecued chicken in the refrigerator and it looked as if he had had a few friends over. I know it was absurd for me to feel left out, but that's exactly what I was thinking. When I asked him about it he said that actually, he cooked it alone. Barbecued alone? Barbecuing is a social thing. The image of Larry outside standing next to the Weber all by himself just killed me. It bothers me still.

Two years passed, we each settled into a new life, got our divorce, Larry found a new girlfriend and they moved to olorado. On June 7, 1980, I was standing on the deck of chard's unfinished sailboat in the middle of our backyard in y satin bridal sailor suit, *and* at the very moment that I was ying "I do," so was Larry. We called each other from our spective wedding receptions and wished each other good ck.

Looking back, I realize I've had two good marriages to two ally good men. I consider myself extremely lucky. Larry has wo teenage daughters and a sailboat now. Richard and I have

Wedding number 1, 1966.

a combo of four kids, three of whom are in their mid-twenti
and all are *un*married.

I'm glad the contemporary standard age for marriage h
changed. Most of the parents I know encourage their kids
wait until they're at least thirty before they take the leap, whi
was the age I was when I took the second leap. It all seems
long ago, and though it's hard to imagine being married
eighteen, it's *impossible* to imagine having sex almost every da
Have I changed!

Prince Charming

You grow up, go to college and then you get married. I never gave much thought that there might be another road to take. I was the ninth of eleven children. I have five brothers and five sisters. We are all alive and no one's in jail. My parents grew up and went to college and got married. My four sisters before me grew up, went to college and then got married. I followed their lead. I always thought I was older than I actually was anyway. I never wanted to be considered flaky or immature. In our house, it was always important to be *mature*. You were rewarded for being *mature*. I went to college, I graduated and thank God I had a boyfriend because . . . it was time to get married.

27

I met Len my junior year in college, living in coed dorm. He was my resident adviser, or my R.A., as they say in colleg speak. He was four years older than I, the perfect marrying ag Though we were both seeing other people at the time, w became friends by staying up late at night discussing the wa we wanted to dump our significant others. We were friend first. Len was the kind of guy who was just charming. He wa a gentleman and he was cute. What really attracted me to hin was his sense of humor. He always seemed to be planning some sort of prank on some unsuspecting resident.

The first time I actually noticed him was Halloween night, when he was dressed as a nun. (I should have seen the Freudian undertones of my Catholic school upbringing drawing me to him like a magnet.) He was with his best friend, Buzz, who was dressed as a bunny. They had come running out of the room of some poor guy who thought he was losing his hair and had come to them in confidence, worried about baldness.

They were laughing hysterically because it really had been the two of them who were putting hair clippings on this guy's pillow in the middle of the night. Len was so tickled with himself that it made the rest of us howl. I called my sister and told her I had met this guy whose name was Leonard Melvin Kristensen Jr. She said, "With a name like that, I hope this guy has some looks."

He does have looks. I fell for him hard. I had struck gold. He, on the other hand, was much more tentative. Always careful to do the right thing, he moved very slowly. He had just graduated and was trying to "find" himself. I didn't see the confusion; obviously he just needed someone to tell him the "master plan." I was the risk-taker. I have a theory that people actually drive as they live. I was in the fast lane, passing all the yo-yos I had dated. He was in the slow lane, taking his time to

gnal before changing lanes. Finally, after months of test-dri-
ng, we became "a couple." I don't think we actually ever
ent on a date. We were together for two years, living three
ours apart. He waited for me to graduate and he proposed to
e on New Year's Eve in Yosemite National Park. We stood in
e middle of a forest in the pouring rain, and he got down on
is knees and asked me to marry him and dropped the solitaire
iamond, a family heirloom, in the mud. I thought that was so
ute and romantic then. If he had done the same thing today I
would have snapped. Funny how the very things that attract
you to someone are all the same things that make you crazy
ater on.

We began planning our August wedding. People thought
we were nuts. People tried to talk us out of it. They said we
were too young. We were sure that this was the right thing. I
had done everything in my life that I could possibly see doing
without him. I knew I had met someone who valued exactly
the same things I valued, who believed the same things I
believed and saw life the same way. He loved food and practical
jokes, what a match. The only thing we would bring to this
marriage would be our education, because neither of us had
any money.

This was going to be the Irish Catholic work ethic wedding.
My older brothers and sisters had gotten married before me
and my mother had painstakingly saved and washed every plastic fork and knife from their receptions. From the time I was
eight years old, I can remember waiting for the guests to leave
and then being instructed to dig through the trash for the plastic cutlery. She then neatly bundled them up in Ziploc baggies
with the count labeled on the outside of the bag. When the
next wedding came along she was careful to buy the exact
brand to match. She had calculated down to the ounce exactly

how much beef and cheese would be consumed by the avera[ge]
American at a wedding reception. Her feeling was, you have [no]
need for a caterer when you have Costco and relatives.

I didn't know any other way, and since Len and I were fre[sh]
out of college we wanted a party that would accommodate [all]
our unemployed friends. You know, all those people that w[e]
can't even name now. Everyone in both our families pitched i[n.]
Len's dad was friends with the chef down on the wharf in Sa[n]
Francisco, who gave him an Italian "deal" on the shrimp. Len['s]
friend Jerry's dad, Guido, was a band leader and he would d[o]
the music. His neighbor, Seb Saia, worked in produce and go[t]
us all the fruit. I went to the flower mart in San Francisco an[d]
I did my own flowers. My mother helped me find the brides[-]
maids' dresses because I was busy taking my finals. Other than
the fact that the morning of my wedding, I was rolling ham
and cheese for the platters, it was sweet. That is, it was
sweet until all the loose ends and the slack that the caterer
picks up slowly began to unravel.

It was the middle of August and hot and muggy in Marin
County, California. I had made myself a beautiful bouquet of
white lilies. The ones with the dusty brown heads on them that
you are supposed to cut off. Well, I didn't know that, and before
the wedding started I had them all over my dress. The dress I
had bought in February when it was cold. It had long sleeves
and enough lace to do a sequel to *Gone With the Wind*. I thought
I would really beat the heat that day by wearing knee-high
nylons under my wedding dress. I even bragged to my bridesmaids about how clever I was. No one thought to remind me
that eventually the garter would have to be removed and then
everyone would know how clever I was.

The passing of time is a cruel thing where weddings are
concerned. I had the underdeveloped taste of a twenty-one-

ear-old and the unfortunate luck of getting married in the arly eighties. When we take out the pictures from that day, othing seems to have survived the test of time. Not the bridesmaids' dresses made of woven ribbon from Montgomery Vard, not the Farrah Fawcett hairdo, and certainly not the rairie-style honeymoon outfit.

My husband wore a light gray tuxedo and posed like a Sears model. My mother wore the Sarah Coventry jewelry that she had won on *Family Feud*. The photographer even took pictures of the food, but the watermelons carved into fruit salad baskets hardly seemed worthy of a place in the wedding album. Yet these are the pictures I'm most proud of.

Then there are pictures I'm not so proud of, and I would say neither are my parents. I hadn't eaten for four days before the wedding because of nerves. My first meal after the stress began to lift was five glasses of champagne. I began to believe I was the blond girl in ABBA. With that many drinks under my belt, no one was willing to argue that I was the "dancing queen." We were all doing a dance that we called "gatoring," which requires excessive shimmying on your back. It tore the bottom five layers of lace from my "Tara"-style gown. I posed on the floor for that photo. I posed for pictures with all my male friends from college with my gown pulled past my thighs to show off the knee-high nylons. You know things were deteriorating when I actually became proud of my widebands. About two hours into the reception I became overwhelmed by alcohol and sentimentality. I blubbered about never seeing my eighty-five-year-old grandmother again, who ended up living for ten more years. My eyes got all red and puffy to match my prairie dress and I posed again. We left the reception to the traditional rice throwing, and I passed out in the car. When I woke up I was in front of the ice cream parlor where my new husband

had treated himself to a double-dip maple cone. The silly thir
is, at that point in the day I still thought the entire affair w:
very classy.

When I look at my parents' wedding photos they seem s
classic and refined. Mine seem so, so . . . disco. It didn't fe
tacky at the time, but looking back, it was a very "Solid Gold
day. I'll never forget, though, the best piece of advice I go

fore I got married. Sister JoAnn, principal at the high school
went to, said to me, "Have a great wedding day but have a bet-
r marriage." She was right . . . and we have! It continues to be
ne one thing that keeps me from having too much remorse
ver such a polyester day.

When the Shark Bites

The key to a long and successful marriage is knowing that it's all about cycles. There's the Honeymoon Cycle, the Irritated Cycle, the Baby-Time Cycle, the Kids Come First Cycle, the I Come First Cycle and the When Is It My Turn? Cycle. Some cycles bring you up and we all try to stay there for as long as we can, but we also know that the inevitable down cycle is just a burnt dinner away. If we can keep our perspective and anticipate the next round of cycles, the loving feelings and intimacy will still be intact when we're finished with another downer.

I wish I had had that knowledge when I first married

ichard. It would have come in handy that day in 1980 when he
spent our last twenty-five dollars on a perm. Instead, I took it
to be a serious infraction of our vows and fashion in general.
That time the down interval lasted about two months, which
was the number of days it took for the perm and me to soften.

A down cycle is a sly entity. Sometimes it begins very quietly.
It can be extremely covert. It might show up right in the middle
of a sentence and last for weeks. Sometimes it will blast in
like a cold wind through the front door and then disappear just
as quickly and dramatically. Other times it will slip in through
a dream. Richard hates it when that happens. We go to bed perfectly
snugly and happy, then, sometime before dawn, I dream
that he's late, irresponsible and a philanderer. I wake up and
give him a disgusted look. He then knows that either I had the
recurring dream or my period came.

Once a down cycle has begun, it takes over my every
thought and action. Like the flu, once you feel that first tickle
in your throat, there's no stopping it from running its course no
matter how much echinecea you take to ward it off. There is no
sex during a down cycle.

Here's a true story demonstrating how it can tarnish a perfectly
happy moment: Richard and I were doing some yard
work on a warm summer afternoon while the kids swam and
the birds sang. He was clipping the trumpet flowers and I was
sweeping the deck when he asked me what I wanted for dinner.
Grateful for his offer and trying to support my latest overweight
consciousness craze, I said I thought fish would be good. I told
him that I would *really like shark*. I said it had been a long time
since I'd had shark and asked him if he could fix it as he had
done last summer. He said he'd like to try a new dill sauce on it
this time. I said I'd make some rice pilaf. It all sounded *really*
good to me. I began to hum "Free Bird" and finished sweeping.

As the sun began to set, I could hear Richard hummin: "Our house is a very very nice house" while he was preparir our meal. It was then that I noticed that there were two kin: of fish in his famous lemon/olive oil/dill marinade. And look ing back, I know I should have used the word "why," even though it was implied when I asked, "You have two kinds o fish?" He answered with a simple, common "yes."

Are you still with me? Because here's where that slippery lit tle down period starts to take off. (I have seen intelligent, insightful psychotherapists fall into this trap. No one escapes from the down cycle!) The *Men Are from Mars* thing began to do its little dance. A woman would have given a sing-songy expla- nation of why there are two kinds of fish in the pan and even given some extra, albeit useless, information about other fish choices and what finally influenced her decision. A man answers the question literally. "There are two kinds of fish?" "Yes." No one is at fault here. It doesn't matter, though, because at this point we all know what's in the immediate future.

My subconscious may have picked up on the down clues, but I paid them no attention and went about my business of setting the table while he tossed the salad. He gave me a little wink. We both started humming "Mack the Knife."

Candles were lit on the patio and Ray Charles was playing on our outdoor speakers while Richard set the garnished plates in front of our respective seats, each with a different kind of fish. The shark was on his plate. Looking at mine, I asked, "What's this?"

"Bottom fish."

"Bottom fish?"

"Yes."

Then I asked suspiciously, "What are *you* having?"

With a bit of defensiveness he said, "*I* was in the mood for ~~sh~~ark."

For a whole minute, I didn't know what to say. This happens *very* rarely to women. I was actually stumped as to which ~~w~~ay to go with it. "Do I let it go? Do I remain confused? Do I ~~c~~all him an idiot?" Although it's not very nice of me, the latter ~~s~~eemed to be a first choice. Now, I know I could have very eas~~i~~ly asked him to share *his* piece of shark with me, but I was up ~~t~~o my waist in the down spiral and shark was no longer the ~~p~~oint.

I could feel it coming on and I really didn't want to fight. Not now. Not with the candles and everything. But I was tingly all over and my brain was electrified with emotions that I didn't know how or where to stuff. Sentences like "Did I not request shark? Did you ask me what I wanted AND did I not say SHARK?" were like sugarplums dancing in my head, along with a couple of "You idiot"s. Feeling grateful that I'm not afflicted with Tourette's syndrome, I knew I needed to purge. I was ready to explode. I thought maybe I could save the romantic moment by quickly dashing inside for a speedy call to Caryl to complain for just a minute, saving all the details for the next morning. I know calling him an idiot is a real bone of contention, but before I could excuse myself I heard my mouth say very tersely, "*I* wanted shark, too."

I think that "you idiot" tone might have leaked out, like Jenny Jones's breast implants, because he countered with, "You NEVER want shark. You should have *told* me you wanted shark."

"I *DID* tell you. *REMEMBER?* I told you that I'd like it if you made it like you did last summer and YOU said you wanted to try your damn dill sauce on it!" The tone coming even stronger. I know because, no doubt about it, I was *definitely thinking,* "What an idiot. What an idiot. What an idiot."

By the time we finished with the "No, you didn't"s and t[.] "Yes, you did"s we were both clearly, almost willingly, spinni[ng] into a down cycle. Voices were raised, accusations were flyin[g] worried children were looking out to the patio to see what w[as] going on, no one was eating shark and Ray Charles was singin[g] "It's Cryin' Time Again." We both started spewing details [of] where we were when one of us said, "I like shark" versus ["I] don't like shark."

The truth of the matter is: I do like shark, but I also like a[ll] kinds of fish and I was touched by his effort and I noticed tha[t] it was such a nice night out. But all of this was lost. Whe[n] you've stepped into a down cycle you don't want to notice nic[e] nights.

For the next few days everything he did irritated me. His everyday habits took on new, sinister meanings. He selfishly moved the car mirrors so he could drive better. This meant that I had to move them back to their original positions at a great inconvenience to me. He fell asleep right in the middle of *The First Wives Club*. He drove too fast when we were trying to find a new street address and painfully slow when we were running late. My jaw began to ache from days of clenching.

Time eventually passes and the down mood wears off, but it's our sense of humor that can speed that process right up. A couple of days later Richard found a toy shark in the kids' room and when the table was set that night, everyone had spaghetti on their plates but me. I had rubber shark. I chided him that even our own President wore a hearing aid and before we knew it we were flirting again. We were lucky that time—it was a short cycle.

I don't think there's anything you can do about those times except maybe acknowledge that the cycle has begun. Hashing over and over again is futile because it's not usually the actual event that causes the fighting. What happens is just the natural cycle of life. Before you get all crazy and start to plot your escape into the Land of the Thin and Divorced, remind yourself about the ups and downs of any relationship. That same fish episode could come up in the middle of one of our up cycles and we'd both be cracking up over how he didn't hear my request. Well, maybe not cracking up.

The Fight

A down cycle is one thing, but every now and then I love a good fight. Unfortunately, a good fight is tough to come by with my husband. He is the middle child in a family of five and he is the only boy. He was born with a stamp on his forehead that reads . . . "Keep the peace at all costs." If a man could be a country, he would be Switzerland. He will say and do anything to keep the peace and maintain the calm.

"How are you today, honey?"

"Oh fine . . ."

"Really, you don't look fine . . . C'mon, what's bugging you? You're pouting."

"Nothing, nothing."

This is so irritating! Every now and then you need to let the lava flow out of the volcano . . . let the sucker blow! We don't fight very often, and frankly, I don't think that is healthy. It's like having good weather all the time—eventually a storm looks pretty exciting. Why do you think people loved *Twister* so much? My Italian friends tell me it's because we don't have the right fighting genes.

I've got to tell you that every now and then I really want a good fight . . . when I'm in the mood, I want it and I want it now. I know exactly what to do and how to stir it up when I really am feeling like Mike Tyson. It's an art that I have perfected after fifteen years of marriage and a thousand afternoons of Oprahs and Donahues. In order to be "right" at the end of the fight, I need an invitation into it, a reason to go at him. We're not talking fists, just a real good verbal sparring. And like sex, I realized that I can only do it well, really well, with my husband. We know the exact words and positions that make it feel good. I feel safe with him and our fighting patterns are well in place. The rules are understood. I can spew and spew and I know he won't leave because that's all it is, spew!

There is nothing like the rush of adrenaline when I can belt out a really hearty and sincere "Who did this? . . . I wanna know right now . . . Who did this? Who left the empty cereal bowl on the couch and then it spilled? Who? Who?"

Then my husband comes running in and says, "All right, all right, I did. I got up to answer the phone and it was an accident. So just calm down!"

"Calm down." The two most explosive words in our family vocabulary. "Calm down." You know what they mean . . . hell, you've said it before yourself. He might as well have said, "You sound just like your mother," because to me, I'm in the mood to fight, my invitation has just arrived and my husband has just left Switzerland.

Ding! Round One.

ROUND ONE: "I do everything! No one else does anything around here and I'm supposed to calm down! How can I calm down?" He leaves me no choice but to go into my "Oppressed Woman Speech." Every woman I know has one. I actually have a friend who, while giving her Oppressed Woman Speech, goes around the house and slams every window shut with the exact cadence of her voice so the neighbors can't hear the raging battle. I admire that kind of suburban brilliance.

The Oppressed Woman's Speech is the speech we will pass on to our daughters; it's every woman's personal Gettysburg Address.

My husband is very quiet for all of Round One, and secretly I know he's just trying to gather his facts and information because he knows Round Two is coming. And how does he know? He knows because he got a small taste earlier this morning when I found out he forgot to mail the house payment a week ago. There wasn't an all-out fight, just a small rumble. It was simply a prelude of things to come. The spilling of the Captain Crunch was simply the match to light the flame.

Round One is generally the part where I back him into our fighting spot. Every healthy married couple has one. It's the place in your house where no one can see you fighting but everyone can hear you fighting. Ours is always where the two counters in the kitchen meet. His parents used to fight in front of the refrigerator, so I figure at least I'm giving him partial advantage by entering his comfort zone. Once we're set, it's time for . . .

ROUND TWO: List anything and everything he has ever done to wrong you, your marriage or your family in any way,

ape or form and back them up with specific dates and exam-
es. "On July 11, 1987, you forgot to pick up the birthday cake
fore the bakery closed." "On September 8 of last year you
id you would hang the mirror in the hallway. It is still not
ne," and so on and so forth.

I find that this is generally where I blow his facts and infor-
ation out of the water . . . because when it comes to infrac-
ons and pettiness I've got a lock on it, and besides, the poor
ing just goes blank. So then, frustrated and/or disgusted, he
lways tries to leave the room . . . and God, I hate that! Don't
ismiss me when I'm arguing with you. Don't you know that I
want to wi— I mean, discuss this with you?

ROUND THREE begins when he turns his back and walks
way. He leaves me no choice but to go for the water power!
There is nothing like a good set of tears to drag a man back
into a fight. By this point I have long forgotten fair fighting. I
just want to win! "Give me a date of the last time you can
remember when I let you down! Give me a date! Ah . . . eh,
ah . . . well, see, you don't know one, do you?"

It's a learned technique for men to hold back for as long as
possible . . . somewhere they were taught, incorrectly, that if
they just hold on this will all blow over. Women give birth.
Believe me, they have all the endurance they need for a good
marital fight.

It's gonna blow, all right. They will snap, it's just a matter of
time, and let's face it, I'm gonna dig until I get it. Don't clam up
on me, 'cause I'm gonna flush it out. I'll follow him around and
wave my arms, I'll get into his car with him if I have to. (It's a
good idea to hide the keys beforehand.)

Please, husbands, don't take all the steam out of this round
by admitting you're wrong too soon . . . because then you'll
ruin it. You see, once a man bails out and says, "I'm sorry,"

that's it, the fight is over . . . you can't keep unloading on
sorry man. A woman who unloads on a sorry man is a bitc
Sorry, girls, but that's the rule. Just do whatever you can to g
him to stay and finish that fight, fairly, of course.

Our fights usually end with us meeting somewhere in th
middle. He says he's sorry and will try to be more helpful, an
. . . well, I agree to limit my list of infractions to a couple o
items next time. He tries to kiss me (not a good move) an
jumps into bed, not realizing that it will be days before I ca
even begin to see him as a sexual being again. Yet I do fee
cleansed, refreshed and ready to face my beautiful life and chil
dren, who are in the next room and are now . . . you guessed it
fighting.

Kids fight very differently than adults. They don't fight over
small unimportant things like cereal stains. They fight over
more important, life-affirming issues. For example: A
popular one at my house is . . . "MOM! He keeps touching me! Make him stop touching me! I asked him very
nicely to stop touching me and he won't leave me alone."

Now, I know that fighting is an important part of growing
up, socializing and getting ready for marriage, but can't you
just get along? All the psychologists say to let them work it out
on their own. That is so hard to do and we all know how well
that worked for Cain and Abel. You see, once I've already satis-
fied my urge to fight, I don't want to hear anybody else satis-
fying their urge.

This kind of fighting, or a modified version of this, can go
on all day long. There are no rules or givens when kids fight.
Anything goes, it gets real ugly and then it's over. One good
swing at each other and then they're back to the kitchen rooting around for Fruit Roll-Ups or Pop-Tarts. They are boys and
genetically they don't know how to do the right thing with the

formation they just learned. They don't know how to document and store it as I do. Then night falls and they climb into bed with smiles on their faces. They couldn't even tell you what the argument was about. Not me! I'm the mom and I'm still stewing about it. "Will they like each other when they wake up or even when they grow up?" "Should I just change their names to Lyle and Eric now and get it over with?"

I'm worried and anxious about them fighting all day, so I climb into bed where I think I can confide in my husband, but he too is now fast asleep. He has long forgotten our fight and their fight. He lies there ever so peacefully with a smile on his face. I begin to look around the room and then I notice an empty cereal bowl on the dresser, and I think to myself, "Yeah . . . tomorrow is going to be a great day!"

Sex and the Married Woman

M

*I*t's hard to be *sexy* when you've been married for a long time. I'm talking about looking, feeling and behaving sexy with the man I married eighteen years ago, the man I truly love. What could be so hard about that? This is the man who will do anything for me. He's there for me when I make mistakes. It's his shoulder I depend on to help me sort out some of the hardest

rts of life. It's his soothing voice saying, "You can do it," that
pires me when I'm the most afraid. This is the man I laugh
d I cry with. This is the man I choose to grow old with.

This also is the man who sees me squirt nasal spray in my
se every single morning. We have semi-meaningful conver-
tions while I clip and paint my toenails, pluck my furry eye-
ows and remove my leg hair. He knows my exact weight, my
a size, the true color of my hair . . . everywhere. He has
eard me sing. And, although I'll deny it, I have passed gas in
ont of him. When you've been married for eighteen years,
nce in a while you've just got to let one rip. Oh, how sexy.

Early love has its ways of protecting us from each other.
When my husband and I first started sleeping together, I did
not hear his bathroom noises. Did he hold them back? Never.
How could I have not heard him blow his nose in the shower?
Clear his throat enthusiastically? When we were first together
and he would be naked with his backside toward me, I would
get a little grin and think, "Yes." Nature begins to take its cruel
toll on all of us after all those years. The other day he was
naked and he leaned way over to pick up the paper and I caught
a glance of his loose body parts and my first thought was, "No,
no." I averted my eyes until the chore was done. I prefer to
keep another, more charming image of him in my head.

I think a well-groomed man is very sexy, it's one of the
things that attracted me to Richard in the first place, but when
I'm present for the grooming process, I have to restart myself
with a good Denzel Washington movie. There's nothing sexy
about watching your man clip his nose hairs with some new
device he's all excited about. Or keep his nice white teeth clean
with the click, click, clicking of the dental floss all during *N.Y.P.D.*
Blue. Now, that's not to say that Mrs. Washington doesn't have
the same problem whenever she walks into the bathroom after

Denzel's had a few chili dogs himself. And you can bet th
she's had to jump-start herself whenever he's been sick w:
the flu for a week, blowing his nose and whining to her. Bu
don't want to dwell on that, then I'll lose *my* fantasy.

I believe it's Mother Nature trying to tell us that we've do:
our job, that is, procreated, and now it's time to stop the co:
tinual humping and concentrate on the raising of our o:
spring. She talks to the women first. Remember when yo
baby was around six months old? Dad comes home from wor
and hints, "Well, honey, it's been about six months. Why don
we put little Mr. Chubby Cheeks in his playpen for a while an
sneak upstairs."

Here's where he tries his big trump card: "Honey, it look
like you could use a nice back rub."

You're tempted, but you know better. You say something
M like "Oh, don't be silly." But you're thinking, "Back rub
my ass! That baby has been sucking on me all day. Don't
you even *think* about it!" Then the baby cries and you
begin leaking. Don't you just want to squirt your husband? I
can't be the only one who's ever tried that.

These days the only thing I want at the end of the day that's
long and hard is a good night's sleep. Isn't it the most irritating
thing when you're lying in bed, nice and ready to drift off, and
you feel that thing poking you in the back? When you've been
married for a while, timing is essential.

Feeling sexy is also essential. I know it's always in the eye of
the beholder, but lately that's been a little elusive for me. I can
no longer take a shower without first steaming up the mirrors
or risk scaring myself. When I was twenty-six, I wore my
sweater and jeans a little tight, just enough to give the viewer
an idea of what might be underneath. Today, I feel an obliga-
tion to the viewer to cover it up.

ree things have to happen before I'm in the mood:

. The dishes have to be done.

2. The homework has to be complete . . . including the biography of Eleanor Roosevelt that's due next week. Otherwise I might yell, "YES! YES! EL-IN-NOOR! EL-IN-NOOR IS AT MY DOOR!" during a hot one.

3. I have to have lost at least one pound. I know one pound is not noticeable. One pound is nothing. One pound is a poop, for God's sake. I don't care who notices it. *I* just need to know it. Then I get all excited and try on my old jeans and realize that I still have nine more pounds to go. Still proud of my weight loss, I'll slip into that Victoria's Secret little string bikini and find that I'm rolling over the whole thirty dollars!

Dressing sexy can put me in the mood. I'm not talking about that thong underwear, either. Those thong things make my hemorrhoids flair up. I can hear them screaming, "Pick a side, will ya? Pick a side!" You've seen those young, shapely things wearing those thongs. Sometimes they wear them when they drop off the kids at school to remind us that they still go to the gym. Didn't their mothers ever teach them to pull stuff like that out? When I try on a thong, I am so uncomfortable, it feels like somebody is going to come up to me and swipe their credit card! No, no, sexy to me is a great pair of shoes and candlelight. I'm not sure my husband has ever really noticed my shoes.

I asked my son Aaron, the expert, who's now twenty-three,

what sexy means to him. I was sure I was going to hear som
thing about long blond hair and was really hoping he'd fin
respectful way of describing female body parts to me. But
told me *flirting* did it for him. Flirting? I was surprised. Wh
pressed for more, he just couldn't come up with another or
Think about that. Flirting is very sexy. Doesn't matter ho
much weight you've gained or lost, even if it's just by going
the bathroom, flirting *is* sexy.

To my amazement, my husband admitted that a *hear
laugh* was extremely sexy to him. Hmmmmm, a hearty laugl
I do that often. Boy, do I feel silly. All those limits I've bee
putting on myself, thinking that sexy was for the young, volu
tuous, thonged single woman with killer shoes when it's bee
right here in my laughter all along. No wonder he wants m
more often on Thursday nights. That's when *Seinfeld* is on.

Up All Night
and Not 'Cause
We Want to Be!

Suddenly a Donut Changed My Life

I graduated from college in May 1982 with a degree in graphic design. I got married in August and by September my husband, Len, and I were apartment managers of a tiny apartment complex in San Diego. We had no jobs, we just wanted to live near the beach. My husband had decided that he wanted to go back to school to get his second college degree, this time in engineering at San Diego State. I had spent about a month dragging my portfolio around trying to find somebod who thought I looked older than twelve to hire me. At twent one, I was married, had a college degree and no experience an was about a week away from going on food stamps. The plac we lived in was so small you could light it with one lamp. Whe someone used the bathroom we used to have to sit on the step outside until the air cleared. The only substantial piece of fur niture we had was his parents' old brown vinyl couch and the glow left over from our honeymoon. Unfortunately the gro cery store wouldn't take brown vinyl and love for food. The only money we had was the money we got from returning the wedding gifts we hated. Electric frying pans were the hot item in 1982. We got eleven of them. We had an old farm truck that we bought for $450 to move our belongings south because it was actually cheaper than renting a U-Haul. This "temporary" vehi- cle became our only car. The fact that we were never sure when it would start didn't bother us, we were newlyweds.

We had been married for about two months when I got a graphic design job working for a medical publishing com- pany. I was hired to draw "disease-ridden" human organs. It wasn't the glamorous graphic design job I had dreamed of, but it was a job. We were poor, and at least drawing gross anatomy nauseated me. I was never hungry and that helped cut down on the grocery bills. After about the second week of work, I start- ed feeling as if I had the flu. Apparently the organs were really taking their toll on me. I would try going to work and kept falling asleep on the drafting table over the sections of kidneys. Early one morning I called my mother, because when you're uninsured and poor, mothers become your primary care physi- cians by default. I said, "Mom, I feel like I have the flu, but the funny thing is, I'm hungry for salad and my hands and fingers feel swollen."

My mother's a high school teacher, a profession she returned after raising eleven children. She was in a hurry that morning and on her way to school. She took a swig of coffee and said, quite nonchalantly, "Well, honey, it doesn't sound like the flu to me. You're probably pregnant, but I'll talk to you later."

I hung up the phone, ran to the bathroom and vomited. My husband stood in the center of our tiny little apartment with his engineering books in hand unable to move for about fifteen minutes. We were both in utter disbelief. "How could that have happened? We were using birth control. I can't be pregnant! We haven't even gotten the proofs back of our wedding photos!" My husband and I hugged in silence and then we cuddled in tears on our waterproof vinyl couch.

We weren't totally convinced I was pregnant, although deep down we knew not to question the diagnosis of a woman who had been through several pregnancies herself. She had been pregnant for eleven years of her life. It makes you miss a period just thinking about it, doesn't it? There was no greater authority. We lived in denial for the first day, hoping for the fever that comes with the flu but not with pregnancy. It seemed with every passing day that the nausea was getting worse. Eventually we had to face it, so I sent Len out to buy the home pregnancy kit. He came into the bathroom, his hands shaking as he passed it to me while I was lying on the floor that had now become my bed. To think that only two months before I had sent him to the store for my favorite perfume that I wore on our wedding day.

The instructions in the EPT kit said that if the results were positive a little pink donut would appear in the test tube within five minutes. We had baked goods in the first thirty seconds. I cried and cried as my husband held me and vowed that it would all be okay. All I had to do was have the baby and he would do

the rest. My sister, who had come over to give us suppo:
threw me a look that said, "The poor thing has no idea ho
much those words will come back to haunt him."

There wasn't even a discussion as to how we would de
with becoming parents. We both wanted children eventuall
Maybe not so soon, but we would take it like adults. Adul
with plans that had to be put on hold. That's what I got fc
marrying a Dane with sperm as fast as Hans Brinker.

I spent the next months retching on the floor of my bath
room. My husband would go back and forth to school ever;
day. He would leave and return with me always greeting hin
from underneath the toilet. I would get the dry heaves so ba(
that I would actually pull a muscle in my rear end that would
spasm, leaving me stranded on the floor. Every now and then I
would drag myself to the vinyl couch for a M*A*S*H rerun and
a change of scenery. As I would crawl back to the toilet, in
the 100-degree San Diego heat, I would inevitably end up
with one of the vinyl couch cushions still stuck to my
back from sweat. I lost fifteen pounds and every time I stood
up, I threw up. Certain smells and tastes became offensive. Dial
soap, Cream of Wheat and tunafish were no longer allowed in
the apartment. Needless to say, I had to quit my diseased-
organ-drawing career.

I spent countless hours on that pink, cold linoleum thinking
about becoming a mother and hoping the day would come
when I wouldn't enjoy all my meals twice. I felt sorry for my
husband. Here he was a newlywed, with his future now looking like a black hole. He never once changed his mind about
me or our baby and he always maintained his sense of humor.
The caring sensitive man that he is . . . bought me a pair of
knee pads for Christmas that year. I think that was his way of
saying, "We're gonna make it."

It was an extremely long winter and spring. My husband dropped out of school, unable to concentrate on being a student and a father. Gradually we let go of our newlywed ways and the dream of living at the beach. We packed up the truck again and headed north knowing that I could get a waitressing job at a friend's coffee shop at night. Len took a job loading produce trucks. We earned enough money to buy a real car. It was a VW Rabbit with a bright red interior. We had transportation. That is, until we discovered that just looking at the red interior caused me to get horrible headaches. There was something about the intensity of the red that just sent my system into overdrive. It was February, I was five months pregnant and still throwing up. We had to cover every inch of the dashboard of the Rabbit with white towels just so I could ride in it.

I was getting depressed, I had to get out. I started to venture into the real world. I was beginning to wonder what it was like to wear something other than a cushion on my back. I didn't feel any better, but I knew getting out might help me to feel less depressed. One of my first adventures was to get cash from the ATM machine. What a big day! I took a shower, put on make-up and drove to the bank. When I got there, the line for the ATM machine was about five-deep. A sense of anxiety came over me. I knew that it was only a matter of time before the wave of nausea returned. I tried doing affirmations and self-talk. "You can handle this . . ." "You smell nothing . . ." As I stood in line in the cold, trying to will it down, the direction of the wind changed and I got a really strong whiff of the cologne on the man in front of me. Before I could move I had thrown up on the back of the man's shoes. They were nice shoes. I tried to clean it off, wiping his shoes and my tears. He thought I was drunk. I wished I was drunk.

This is why I have a really hard time with my friends who

enjoy being pregnant. When it comes to beautiful pregna
women I am extremely bitter. They look like glowing summ
fruits; I retained more water than the Hoover Dam and al
wanted to do was kill the person who designed those dress
with the huge bows on the front! When will they learn .
whales and bows don't mix? I looked like a damned gift in th
maternity wear of the eighties.

I had a sister-in-law who was pregnant at the same time an
I couldn't help comparing myself to her. She had a beautiful li
tle belly that sat on top of her long skinny legs. I realized fo
the first time that there are only two kinds of pregnan
women, the cows and the fruits. The fruits feel well enough to
brush their hair and put on makeup. The cows like mysel
seem to worsen their situation by doing things out of shee
desperation. Things like deciding in the seventh month that I
should have been a redhead—with a perm! Even the
fathers in the presence of fruits are much happier people.
They are "co-fruits," proud to comment on and even display their glowing spouses. The "co-cows," like my husband,
are protective at best. They keep their distance, wisely, always
measuring the psychological temperature of their heifers. They
move slowly in their presence and are always prepared with a
plastic bag and a roll of paper towels.

By the seventh month the true meaning of "cow" came into
play. I had stopped throwing up after ten in the morning and
gained a renewed interest in food. In the next two months I
gained an extra twenty-five pounds from my uncontrollable
grazing. There was nothing graceful about it. It was ugly and
all my husband could do was stand back and watch. As soon as
the morning nausea would stop I would plow through every
carbohydrate I could get my hands on, stopping only to smell
the milk that I was washing it down with.

The "glowing summer fruits" labor differently, too. Their labor is always textbook. Under one hour and clean. They certainly won't say an unkind word to their husbands during labor. Their cheeks flush, just enough to look as though they've put on makeup. They will go through labor all naturally and then they will wear their prepregnancy jeans home.

With us cows it's all ugly and messy. I screamed at everybody as they ran for cover. I felt my true self leave my body as a thrashing alien emitting guttural, tribal sounds took over. I had to share a room with a woman who had been in labor for three days. She had brought with her an entire entourage of people who looked like dirty little Ewoks. Let's just say they ate a lot of granola. This woman was bound and determined to have that baby naturally. Her

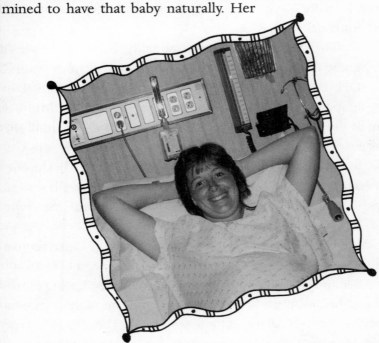

Smiling through the fifth "Hippie Dilation Evaluation."

friends were trying to get gravity to work for her by walkir
her up and down the hallway. Every time a contraction cam
she tore down another doorjamb with her bare hands. A frien
of hers was giving the baby's father a massage in the bed ne>
to me. Well, I watched her for eight hours just screamin' an⟨
ripping the skin off her husband's face! That kid was not com
ing out. I'm sure it took one look at that group, who by the way
kept checking her dilation, in front of my husband, and said
"No way . . . I ain't going home to that commune." It was ⟨
psychedelic nightmare. I noticed the anesthesiologist pacing
outside my door. I called him in, grabbed him around the
throat and pulled him close to me and said, "I just want you to
know . . . I will do any drug you give me." I have to tell you,
when I finally got it . . . that epidural was better than the sex
that got me there.

Then the doctor came in and said, "Caryl, things aren't
going fast enough. I'm gonna have to break your water."
OH, BONUS! Well, she came in to do that and her arm
just disappeared. I was thinking to myself, "Did she lose her
arm at the elbow or is it where I think it is?" I didn't think she
was ever coming back. Then my husband (the caring sensitive
one), the entire time all of this is happening, is over in the corner having a cup of coffee and a croissant . . . He swallows and
says, "Honey, do you need any help?" This from the man who
said, "All you have to do is have the baby!"

Well, by the time the anesthesiologist had managed to give
me the epidural, it was too late and I had to have a C-section.

After an agonizing nine months of no money, feeling crum-
my and bad luck, we had a son. Of course, no words can ever
describe the immediate and intense love that you feel for your
child. He was perfect. In that instant, life was perfect. Everyone
told me that I would forget the pain and hardship of the preg-

ncy. They were wrong. I wrote it down so that I wouldn't
rget, because even at twenty-one I was smart enough to
now that childbirth is something worth remembering ...
ecause when you forget ... you get pregnant again.

Honey, May I Ask a Small Favor of You?

*W*hen I was thirty-eight I had decided that I wanted another baby. I would see other mothers nursing and I'd begin to swoon. I was pitifully fawning over puppies. I would sway when I held things. It seemed like everyone in the 'hood had either newborns or plump little drooling toddlers. My boys were already ten and eleven years old and I was forcing them to sit on my lap. I wanted a plump little drooling toddler, too. I wanted a drooling *girl* this time and I wanted her right away! I became a woman on a mission for sperm.

The only problem was my husband. Or maybe it was the vasectomy I made him get before we were married. Oh, chard is such a big baby when it comes to having his genitals orked over. What is it with men and pain in their crotch anyay? They're so sensitive. We women have been peeked at, oked at and probed for centuries. You would think we were e Discovery Channel, for God's sake. You should have seen m cringe at the very thought of a vasectomy. He just couldn't ear anything made of steel coming near his little tender unit. said, "Honey, they're just going to snip a little tiny piece of our wiring out of your little tiny scrotum. It's not like some vet, squirmy, eight-pound, six-ounce, bulging thing is going to lowly work its way out of your personal area. Calm down."

He bravely got his vasectomy and then a few years later, I requested that he get it reversed. Oh, come on, it's not as if I was asking him to clean out the garage or anything. I just wanted him to get a common, ordinary reverse-ectomy. I teased, "Honey, it will be fun! I'll go with you. I could feed you ice chips, you could beg for drugs. I can see it now, you with your legs spread *wide* apart and every little hair will be standing on end. And when that mean old doctor comes at you with that big, sharp, *steel* knife, I'll remind you to breathe. Hey! We could videotape it! There you'll be all hot and sweaty, your hair all stuck to your face. But you'll still be beautiful to me! Come on, what do you think? Let's do it! I promise I won't ask for anything else ever again."

While he was in surgery getting his vasectomy reversed, I was downstairs at the drugstore buying my ovulation kit and my basal thermometer. I figured, while my husband was recovering from the reconstruction, I could be learning exactly when I was laying my egg. I had just read that in order to conceive a girl, you had to do it right at ovulation. Doggie-style. Now, I was not going to challenge *Redbook*'s authority on those matters. I was sure I wanted a girl.

Don't get me wrong, I truly love my boys. There's nothi
in the world like those energetic, jump-right-in-the-pudd
kindhearted, fearless beings. There's such a spark of tendern
between a mother and her son. I feel sorry for anyone wl
can't appreciate the sweet wholesomeness of little boys. The
are precious. However, I didn't always understand their beha
ior. When my boys were little, they'd go to a drawer, put the
hand in the drawer, *slam it,* then come cry to me. I would con
fort them. Then they'd go *back* to the drawer, put their hand i
it, slam it and come crying to me again. I'd just stare at then
and ask, "Do you get it? Do you get it? It's going to hurt EVER'
TIME." I wanted a child with *all* her chromosomes this time.

Besides, I needed some company. Do you know what it'
like to live with three beefy males? Let me ask you a question
here. Do you think passing gas is funny? Every time? Oh, on

M any given night they would be cutting them, laughing,
imitating them, laughing, lighting them, laughing. It's the
House of Gas Club. But if I should let one little bubble
slip out, they're horrified and everyone yells, "MOM!"

One more thing . . . boys spit. I wanted a girl.

So finally, one chilly morning, on January 19, 1985, at 11:45,
I felt my egg release. What perfect timing. It was a Saturday
and Richard was coming home from work at noon. So I slipped
into a pair of special Frederick's of Hollywood, mail-order,
guaranteed-to-get-you-pregnant, baby pink, crotchless panties
and started singing The Captain and Tennille's "Do That to Me
One More Time." My egg was out of the gate and I was ready!

One should never combine the concepts of crotchless
underwear and motherhood. Try not to visualize it. If my boys
had popped into that room, as they had a habit of doing, they
would have been scarred for life. As it was, I had to throw on a

obe and fix them lunch. Have you ever made a peanut butter
nd jelly sandwich in crotchless underwear? It's wrong.

While I was waiting for my Sperm Machine to come home,
threw in a load of wash, tried some new body lotion, gave the
dog a flea pill, wrote out some bills, put flower petals in our
bed, picked up the G.I. Joe Battle Station, gave myself a breast
check, cleared the dishwasher and threw a Weight Watcher's
Chicken Enchilada Suisa in the microwave. The crotchless
underwear was beginning to irritate me.

By five o'clock that night I was in tears. The phone rang. It
was my neighbor Barbara. I was sounding a little like a twisted
Laura Petrie when I sobbed, "Oh, Barb. I've been waiting all
day. I'm sick of wearing these stupid pink crotchless underwear. My egg is loose. I need to do it now! Doggie-style." After
a slight pause she said, "Do you want me to send Sam over?"

What a good neighbor! It's what suburbia is all about. And
we had lent each other so much already that I even hesitated
for just a split second. (I told you I was a woman on a mission.)
But Sam was way too hairy and I wanted a girl and all. I couldn't
risk it. I thanked Barb for her thoughtful offer and finished
doing the laundry.

By the time my Richard got home, the pink lace around the
edge of those damn panties had rubbed me raw. I was in no
mood for sex. I figured we could try next month.

The next day was the Super Bowl. The San Francisco 49ers
were playing the Miami Dolphins. It was a great game. The
boys and their dad were at their happiest. I love the music of
the family. There were many hours of cheering, laughing,
good-hearted teasing, eating nachos and, of course, another
day in the House of Gas. I was feeling mighty grateful for what
I already had. I must say, watching Joe Montana all afternoon

had put me back in the mood. That night in bed we celebrate our sweet life, the 49ers and Joe Montana . . . (Go Joe!)

Well, that celebration launched another. My daughter eleven now and she's been such a blessing. I got myself female companion. We like the same movies, we speak the same language, we shop. I got everything I expected from a girl and a little more. You see, having had her big brothers as mentors, I should have known that my dainty little double X chromosome buddy would have mastered the fine art of gas entertainment. I'm so proud. The other day she came up to me and said, "Mommy, why does Daddy keep slamming his hand in the drawer?" I gave her a little kiss on the top of her head and said, "Oh, you'll be finding that out in science class this year."

Drip, Drip, Drip . . .

*T*here was something about bringing the baby home that was so frightening. I begged to stay in the hospital for just a few more days. I was too healthy—they made me go. I knew the minute I got home I would be on my own. I saw the puzzled and raw look of my husband as we signed the release papers. Sure, it was a shock to his system to have to write a check for $2,000 for that uninsured C-section, but there was fear under there, too. He had never been around an infant before. This was gonna take some time. Little did I know that it would not be until the birth of our next child that he would feel comfortable.

I was breast-feeding and my body was making enough mi
for me to feed the entire neighborhood. Remember, I was on
of the cows. Our son Bryce never wanted the bottle. He wou
rather go hours without food than suck on that rubber nipple
Even if I had attempted to pump out his favorite brand, ther
was no way he was going to settle for latex. He was also a littl
piranha when he got back to the breast, so of course tha
would just cause me to make more milk. We tried every
thing . . . no, I take that back . . . I tried everything. Breast-feed
ing became mentally and physically incarcerating. I coulc
swear to you that that baby was sucking out every bit of intelligence I had in my brain. Even Erica Kane's life started looking
really good to me. Seven marriages, hooked on prescription
drugs, losing her hair to a rare disease . . . I could handle that,
at least she's not dripping. Every orifice in my body seemed to
run for weeks. I had pads for everything. Pads for the
bleeding, pads for the nipples, pads for the hemorrhoids.

My husband tried a few times to intervene, but I wouldn't
let him. I was so hormonal that I had absolutely no patience to
allow him a learning curve. He always seemed to move in slow
motion. That baby could be projectile-vomiting and I'd be
screaming for a diaper. It would take him twenty minutes to
bring me a useless disposable diaper! Then he'd look at me and
say, "What . . . what'd I do wrong? . . ." He didn't get it. He had
zero common sense where this baby was concerned, and I had
zero tolerance for his clumsiness.

I read everything I could get my hands on during that period
of my life. T. Berry Brazelton, Penelope Leach, these were my
heroes and mentors. If I didn't know it, I asked about it or read
about it. Not my husband; he was more willing to guess. I
found that guessing was never helpful at two in the morning
when your breasts were about to explode from engorgement. I

ink men are just too separated from the physical process. After all, their breasts don't have to be bound up with receiving blankets. I know he cared, but it was as if he didn't want to get dirty or was simply intimidated by the devil he was living with. It must have been ruining his whole fantasy of what those days were supposed to be like for him. The worst part was the moments when he would try to be funny . . . a quality I used to admire in him. Well, nothing is funny when you're entering the postpartum period. My little comedian always tried to slink out of the problem by making some little joke. I wanted to kill him, but I needed him to run to the store for more pads.

We had been given about four baby showers before Bryce was born. We had every piece of equipment known to baby. These were the things that were supposed to make our lives easier, but if you want to see a sideshow, put your husband out on the driveway, with one of those fancy strollers that folds down to fit in your purse, and ask your husband to "open it." It was so fun to watch this very smart man have such a hard time. (I know it sounds cruel, but I was experiencing so little joy myself . . .) It would take him about fifteen minutes to figure it out and by then it was time to sit down and breast-feed again.

The swing was a godsend. Motion, motion, it was all about motion. The only drawback was that when Bryce was born they only had the crank-up kind. You got a maximum of fifteen minutes of peace, tops. When the swing stopped my husband used to try stealthily to crank it up again. That loud screeching of the crank would send Bryce into hysterics. He'd start flailing his little arms and legs and get all caught up in his blankets. I was so jealous when they came out with the battery-operated model. It was too late for us. The new ones can go 150 hours on one D battery. In that amount of time you could go away

for the weekend and come back. Do you think that would ^
considered child abuse?

The hardest part of this early time in your child's life is th
everyone expects you to be enjoying it. I wanted someone ^
pull me aside and say, "We know you love that little guy, no^
go ahead and open your window and scream . . . 'Who are ^
kidding? I'm exhausted and this sucks!' "

Touch the Clouds, Heather

*W*hen our infant son could finally hold his head up, my husband and I raced to the park. We just couldn't wait to have a child who actually did things other than poop and cry for food. Never mind that it took big blankets to prop him up in that swing. We had waited a long time to take our baby to the park, and so what if he didn't know the park from his crib, we did. We would look over jealously at the kids playing in the sandbox and swinging unassisted, wanting desperately to hurry him up. I said to my husband, "Won't it be fun when Bryce plays in the sand and can go down the slide on his own?" It still amazes me how much I didn't see from the other side of the

fence! You know, the fantasy side of the fence was much bette
than the reality side. By the time he was old enough to sit up i
a swing I had another child and was sitting squarely on th
exhaustion side of the fence. I had a newborn and a three-yea
old. Bryce was not playing in the sand, he was eating the sand
I'm sure now that the other child was, too, but I lived in tha
fantasy that all first-time parents do. Over the years I've had t
stop myself from constantly ruining other people's nirvana.
had become the very person I hated to hear when my kids were
young, never missing a moment to point out that the good stuf
doesn't last for long. "Oh, you better enjoy it, 'cause pretty
soon they'll be biting each other," or "They won't be little forever, you'll turn around and he's going to be a teenager with a
bad attitude." I suppose ignorance of your child's next phase is
really the only thing that gets you through the first child,
because if we'd known we would've tried to give them
back on occasion.

We've all had days when we are so tired that going on
seemed impossible. When you are caring for little ones you
pray for little things. Things like nobody saying the word
"Mommy" for two minutes or to get out in the evening *alone*
carrying *just* a purse. It didn't matter where I went, just that I
got out. Often my destination was just wandering through
Target, checking to see if the sweats had come in in any new
colors. The more mindless the trip, the better.

When I was really tired, the park seemed the perfect remedy.
I could let Bryce loose, put the baby in the stroller and collapse
on a bench like a homeless person. One day at the park when
my kids were about two and five years old, there was a woman
there with her four-month-old daughter propped up in the
swing. I noticed her pushing her daughter and talking to her
in that high, squeaky tone used by a mother who hasn't yet

ccumbed to exhaustion. She kept saying, "Touch the clouds, eather, touch the clouds, baby girl . . . make a rainbow for Iama . . ." To which I could only gag under my breath. "Oh, nuuuut up. Heather is going to be teething and slamming oors on those clouds any time now." Oh my God, I had ecome a pessimist. My kids aren't that bad. They are, after all, ust kids. I kept trying to move to another spot in the play- ;round, away from "Nirvana Mommy," but, like a magnet, my)ersonal "princess of pain attitude" kept ending up in the same)lace on the playground as she. Now we were over by the slide, where my son proceeded to go backward up the slide and throw sand from the top of the slide onto little Heather. Nirvana Mommy then sat Heather in the sand and began to sing Raffi songs to her. I could have kept my mouth shut, but nooo, I had to say it. "My son ripped all the tape out of the cassette on our copy of *Baby Beluga* when he was two." I just couldn't give her those moments.

What was wrong with me? I was tired and feeling so sorry for myself that I guess I wanted her to be miserable, too. I wanted to tell her that Heather would probably be a bitch just because she was named Heather. I must have been in an espe- cially foul mood that day because I started enjoying my nega- tivity far too much. I finally got the strength just to pack up and leave before I started to make Nirvana Mommy cry. I wiped the sand off my kids and strapped them into their car seats, using the crowbar grip required to subdue their arching backs. After two minutes, they had fallen asleep in their car seats and I ended up in the drive-through line at McDonald's. We had to keep moving. I ordered Happy Meals. The employee who took my order was a gray-haired woman in her sixties. As she handed me the food, she peeked around at my sleeping chil- dren and she said to me, "That is so sweet . . . enjoy it. My son

left his wife and three kids with no money, they live with m
and that's why I'm working here now."

It was now four in the afternoon. I walked in the doc
loaded down with equipment and babies and the smell c
McDonald's on my shirt. I dropped everything and began t
cry. Thankfully, my husband had come home early from wor
and was there to relieve me. He put *me* down for a nap. A lon
and glorious nap.

When I woke up, I felt like a new person. I made dinner
bathed the kids and got them ready for bed, all done with a
really good attitude. As I tucked Bryce in, he was asleep before
his head hit the pillow. I was overcome with guilt. I love my
kids more than life itself. Why did I have all those nasty
thoughts? Nirvana Mommy was probably even a better mom
than me. I kissed his cheek and whispered in his ear,
"Tomorrow we'll go to the park and Mommy will push you in
the swing so you can touch the clouds, too. 'Bitter Mommie'
had a nap and she is all gone now."

Carpool Diem—
Seize the Ride

Boys & Girls & Girls & Boys & Boys & Girls

*L*ast September the noon news showed a piece about the common challenges teachers face with little boys and little girls. The newscaster reported that boys often have poor penmanship, have trouble sitting still and cause disruptions with fighting. Little girls are often timid, are unhappy if they can't sit close to one another and have physical complaints without known cause.

Now, I perked up when I heard that last one because just that very morning Marcy had pointed out that if she wrinkled up her nose "it really hurts."

My answer was stating the obvious: "Then don't wrink[
your nose, honey."

That evening, after I tucked her in and kissed her goo[
night, she stalled my exit by complaining that her shoulder hu[

"It'll be okay, sweetheart. Good night. I'll see you in t[
morning." The morning came with sore legs from PE. "Th[
happens when we use muscles we haven't used in a long tim[
Now get ready for school."

God forbid she breaks her wrist or something. I'd be force[
to say, "It's just fine, honey, now go to sleep."

*W*hen it comes to hypochondria, little girls do not have it
cornered. I live with a child who would like nothing
more than to get a neck brace as a birthday gift. It's finally
beginning to wane now, but for a while there we owned more
splints and knee braces and crutches than most hospitals. Every
hurt, every pain had to be the sign of a major injury. He was
darn good at the acting part, too. Before we caught on, he had
us back and forth to the doctor ten times. We weren't slow, we
just didn't want to be reprimanded if there happened to be
something really wrong with him. After the x-rays showed
nothing and Bryce got a little sympathy from some unsuspecting nurse, we would usually leave the doctor's office with a
sling or some other injury accessory. When we went shopping,
I used to have to plead with him to remove his equipment so

people wouldn't jump to incorrect conclusions after seeing a five-year-old on crutches wearing a neck brace with a sling on his arm. This is my fault, isn't it? Did I miss that child development chapter? I wondered where I went wrong. Was it because we were careful not to baby him when he got hurt and now he needs attention? Or is it because in his little head he saw someone else showered with attention from an injury and thought, 'That's easy . . . get the brace, get some love.'"

The only other possible theory is that this whole thing was not unlike participating in yet another sport. As with all sports, the sport of being injured required lots and lots of equipment. We all know that the better equipment a player has, the better he is at the sport. Right?

One winter there was a horrible cold going around, everyone we knew had it. I went in early one morning to wake Bryce for school and he rolled over and said in a most pathetic voice, "Mommy, my head hurts and I have a sore throat." Well, I immediately suckered in, rationalizing that "It was going around . . ." and "Besides," I thought, "I'll give him an extra dose of that Triaminic and it'll be a quiet day." Oh, come on, we all know, they're so good when they're sick . . .

Well, he would have been if he had *truly* been sick. Everywhere I went in the house that day I could hear his little pitter-patter behind me. In order to get him to keep up the game, I would say, "How are you feeling, honey . . ."

To which he would muster up in his best fake sore throat voice, "I'm feeling a little better."

After a morning of this charade I tried to bust him. "C'mon, Bryce, you're not really sick, are you . . . ?"

Not one to go down without a fight, he would put the histrionics into full gear. He would start coughing and sniffling and really working it up and then say, "See? I am sick."

To which I could only say, "Yeah, then if you have a col[d] why are you limping?" Gotcha!

He's fourteen and every now and then I'll open the cabin[et] in the boys' bathroom where the pile of slings and braces ar[e] stored and just giggle. He's pretty much given up on gettin[g] our unwarranted sympathy anymore. Unfortunately, his pas[t] still follows him. This boy cried wolf so many times that i[f] something should really happen to him, they're going to hav[e] to show me photographs, depositions and blood sample[s] before I write a single check to a doctor.

*H*aving had kids who represent each gender, I've noticed some unique characteristics. While both have healthy, active imaginations, each goes about fulfilling that potential in decisively opposite ways. One hot summer day, the neighborhood kids, ages seven, eight and nine, were all swimming in our pool. I observed that the little girls would swim more often in the shallow end. They were pretending they were otters. There was a mommy otter and two sister otters. The mommy otter was teaching her children how to swim on their backs with clams on their chests. Meanwhile the boys were seeing how far into the middle of the pool they could jump. I heard an inventive Billy exclaim, "I know, I'll fart!" Apparently he thought his gas would propel him farther into the pool.

I noted how this quality plays itself out in the classroom

ring art class. The teacher brought in lots of junk: little wood ocks, empty spools of thread, tin foil, pipe cleaners and so on, d a glue gun. The assignment was to make some sort of ace vehicle. The boys' pieces were huge, with most of the oncentration going toward elaborate weapons on the front ortion. The girls' vehicles were of small to moderate size, ith complicated color patterns of "lights" made out of but- ons circling the ship. Lucy was fixated on making little cur- ains for the little windows and Lola discovered some fabric hat made a "perfect carpet." I pointed this out to another parent- elper and she simplified it for me: *Boys want to obliterate while girls want to decorate.*

*B*oys want to obliterate is right . . . what boy do you know who doesn't turn every object into a gun? From the moment they were born everything became a gun . . . Legos, sticks, blocks, even their own penises in the bathtub (and they say there's no connection between that member and power).

I tried to direct them away from violence, and the harder I tried the more they craved the ninja lifestyle. They longed to be Superman and Spiderman and Batman. They wore pajamas with capes that became streetwear. The motivation to play with building blocks was fueled only by the joy of tearing them down. This is clearly a gender thing.

It has always been about guns and balls in our house. If you

can't blow it up or bounce it, there is no point in owning it
would only notice it when a friend would come over with h
daughter. My boys used to line up all their action figures in
row and one by one shoot them down with some ball-lik
object, while at the same time making elaborate sound effect
They especially loved to act out dying themselves. We didn
have too many cross-gender toys, so when the girls came ove
to play, they would line up the same action figures and pos
them in friendly noncombat positions with their acces
sories/weapons displayed all pretty, like in a Nordstrom's win
dow. I tried giving the boys dolls. They simply became
hostages, so I gave up and gave in. Maybe that's why they are
so comfortable living in rooms that resemble war zones now.

*A*s I watch my daughter grow, I notice how some of the
stronger traits in women manifest themselves early on.
For example: There's the time when the neighborhood kids
were all playing and I asked why the girls kept marching in
from the front yard to the office and then back out again.
Marcy reported, "We're keeping a list on the computer of
every time the boys are rude; on the tenth rude thing, we print
it and give it to their parents!" Men just don't stand a chance.

Even now, when I ask Marcy about school she'll go into
long stories about how Paul got in trouble for not singing and
how she didn't think it was right because she noticed that Paul

asn't himself all day and could be coming down with some-
ing. She'll describe with sympathy how her friend Julia was
aving a hard day because she was upset about her parents'
ivorce. She reported that her friend liked both houses, but
ulia's room at her father's house was real big with only a little
it of furniture in it and she felt lonely in there. On the other
and, her dad had a really cute dog. Marcy commented to me
hat she's glad her room is on the small side. In these two exam-
les Marcy observes, communicates, gives her opinion, prog-
osticates and sympathizes. When I ask my boys how school is,
they reply, "Okay," and no amount of prodding gets me more.

The first time I ever flew first-class I had to meet Caryl in
Cleveland, so I traveled alone. There was only one other person in the cabin, a very nice woman with a gauze bandage over
one eye. By the time we took off, I knew about her son's problem in third grade, her husband's midlife career change and
what she wanted in the way of new curtains for the living
room. As we traveled across the plains, she heard about my
breast reduction, Richard's vasectomy reversal and what drugs
I requested during childbirth. Just before we landed she
explained that she had to wear that patch for a few weeks
because she had gotten an aneurysm from masturbating. She
explained that at the moment of orgasm a blood clot was
released and somehow went to her eye. I wished her good luck
and we both went our own ways. My husband flew up north
last week and when I asked him how the flight was, he replied,
"Okay."

Communication isn't the only thing that demonstrates our
gender differences. Let's talk about priorities, see if you've ever
been in this situation. Marcy's seventh birthday plans were
elaborate. Parents were to drop off their children at 1:00; by
1:15 Richard and I, each in separate cars, were to drive the kids

to Great America Amusement Park, arriving at approximately 2:00. We were scheduled for "The Party Room" from 2:15 ti 2:45, when the Caseman family would take it over for littl JoAnna. At around 12:50, Richard took his car to get gas. waited, paced, tapped my foot and stood at curbside with eigh anxious children until 1:30.

Trying, but *not* succeeding, to contain my frustration an temper, I asked, "What the hell took so long?" He explained that he did get the car gassed, but decided to have it washed and on the way home he stopped very quickly at a garage sale. He then showed me his bargain: a little round silver ice bucket with penguins embossed on the sides. Apparently he hadn't noticed that it was identical to the one we just got rid of at our garage sale.

What made him forget the time schedule of the party? What could possibly have gone through his mind? Did he say to himself, "I realize that I should get right back, kids are waiting for me, but the car's exterior is so darn unsightly this way"? And, "Look! A garage sale! Wouldn't it be something if I found Marcy a birthday present here, right now? Would ya look at that ice bucket! I bet we could use one of these at home!"? I know I sound like a condescending, irritated wife. There are some that would readily use the word "bitch" here, but I don't think a female dog could be as pissed off as a wife.

*I*t certainly seems that women and men, and boys and girls, have a very different approach to life. I wish I could find a way to understand theirs without feeling . . . sort of . . . well . . . superior. Are they tuning us out or do they really not get it sometimes? In the relationships that my boys have there seems to be so little expectation from their friendships. A simple grunt hello means "We are still friends, and if we aren't there's always another soldier who will be." The subtleties of relationships are lost on them. I always try to butt in and attempt to be the bridge, filling in with the details I feel are so desperately needed to keep the friendship alive. For instance, when one of Bryce's friends calls, the two of them are on the phone no more than thirty seconds with each other. It takes longer to clear your throat. I always say, "How's Evan doing, Bryce?" He replies, "Fine, I guess."

That's it . . . how do you build a friendship on "Fine, I guess"? They would rather make ten thirty-second phone calls than have to be tortured with a free-flow conversation of five whole minutes.

Now the girls are starting to call, and by the sounds of the conversations, the girls are far more astute in using the phone as a tool. The phone to girls is like the guns were to the boys, pure power. The other day a group of eleven-year-old girls called and asked Eric, "What are you wearing?"(an attempt to be provocative, if there is such a thing at eleven). Obviously they had picked up on some *Melrose Place* phone flirting scene.

Well, Eric had no idea, nor did he care, why they would a[...] such a stupid question. He answered simply, "Basketball shor[...] and a T-shirt, why?"

When you think about it, that's a lot of marriages in a nu[...] shell. He was not picking up on it at all. His wiring just wasn[...] allowing him to go there. The girls, on the other hand, have a[...] these illusions and fantasies that they have spent hours workin[...] on before they even made the call. These girls are actually con[...] ferencing three people in at once these days. "Who likes whom" is going around the class at lightning speed. Little do they know it's wasted on the boys, who have no clue what's happening inside those female heads. If only I could be young again. They are ruling the world from one eleven-year-old's bedroom.

We girls can talk for five hours on the phone. Sometimes at the end of an evening my ear is actually all red and sore, as if someone had literally been chewing on it. The best thing that ever happened to technology was the home headset that clips to my belt. Why, if it wasn't for the phone I would have no friends at all, no life and no career. My husband, wouldn't you know . . . is the only man who falls under this phone-loving category. He's really a mutant in that way. He loves to chat so much that even my girlfriends have to cut him off to say, "That's good, Len . . . now give the phone to Caryl." Yet even though I'm married to a chatterer, I still put money on the fact that most men fall into the grunt-and-go category.

There is nothing like the "raising boys versus girls" topic to get parents all fired up. Now, we all know there are certain things that fall right down very gender-specific lines. It's only when we get backed into a corner that we are not willing to admit to them. It's either that, or our need to defend the weak-nesses in our children. I have a friend with three boys and noth-ing sends her like an offhanded remark like "I can't believe your

use is so clean with all those boys!" To her this is not a comment but a slam. To me it would be a compliment. They *are*
essy when left to their own devices. Yes, there are men who
e clean and neat and tidy, but I bet you it was because they
ere well trained by a woman.

The assumption is that we are not happy living only with
oys that gets under my skin. I actually had a neighbor who
ropped by with her daughter in her first communion whites
imply to say, "See what you'll be missing."

I thought, "How dare she assume that I am pining away for
daughter." I'm perfectly happy raising two boys and I don't
eel the need to go out and get my husband's sperm spun to get
a daughter. I always knew I would have boys. I told my husband
before we got married that we would have only boys. They say
God gives you what you can handle, well, I'm low on patience
and doubt I could've handled a smaller version of myself. I
admit there are days when I need to get out with some gentle
non-wrestlers, days when I need some female bonding, but I do
love being the only girl around. I love being needed and adored
for the gentleness I bring to their lives and I love the raucous
wild behavior they bring to mine.

Boys become men and men have a much better "bigger picture" philosophy than women. They don't get bogged down in
the details of living and this in turn makes them much more
efficient. They also plow ahead never checking the temperature of "feelings" and "emotions" the way we girls do. I read
somewhere that it's because of this that men actually raise
much more independent children. We mothers are constantly
stepping in to fix everything, never leaving anything to be discovered or learned, and then wonder why we are surrounded
by ineptness. I hate to admit it, but it is our own damned fault.
You'll never see my husband running a water bottle out onto

the football field. You'll never see him bringing a jacket to o
sons when the weather turns cold. He rarely makes scho
lunches, and if he makes them at all, it's not very well, so th
boys learn they are better off doing it themselves rather tha
having the jelly running out of the sandwich and making th
Baggie all sticky. I would rather die than make a sandwich lik
that.

The best thing Marilyn and I ever did for our children wa
to go out on the road. They learned to survive without us
Without mother hen there to coax and prod, backpacks and
lunches were going off to school without reminders. In fact
I'm doing a lot more running around these days . . . I'm starting to think it's time to go out on the road again. Men are just
plain better at training for independence. Now, whether or not
they do it intentionally is a whole other story, and I'm certainly
not willing to give them credit for that.

Little League

AMERICA
THE BEAUTIFUL!

Little League.

Ours is an athletic family. We love sports. We love to watch them, play them and coach them. I grew up with five brothers and five sisters, all of whom played something. There is nothing quite as fun as being on a team even if you're only warming the bench. It was in the spring, at the Little League field that we had our own wonder years. I have great memories of light and sunny afternoons at the ballpark where the boys all played, motivated by the possibility of a free Sno-Kone if they won that day. The girls watched and did laps back and forth from the snack bar. Licorice was ten pieces for a quarter, and we kept score on wooden pegs in the outfield. We rode our stingray bicycles as fast as we could to the field, with our mitts looped around our handlebars. We had stability and independence and stomachaches from all the junk we ate.

Then I grew up, got married and had two sons. I looked forward to them playing all kinds of sports. I brag to my boys all the time about my athletic prowess. They say, "But Mom, you don't run very fast, how could you have been good?" So they force me into explaining that before my butt got big from having them, I actually was a darn good athlete myself. My husband was a very successful athlete, too. If it hadn't been for the fact that he was blind without glasses, he might have had an opportunity with a major-league team. We couldn't wait for our sons to play . . . thankfully, when they were old enough to play Little League they actually wanted to. Whew!

When my first son played Little League, we were living in Petaluma. Licorice prices had gone up to three for a quarter, but the big attraction on opening day was still the hokey little parade through the downtown while the World War II veterans' band played off-key and the mayor threw out the first ball. Our oldest son, Bryce, played in Petaluma for three years. We all came to love the smell of spring. It meant baseball.

When we moved to Los Angeles my boys were ten and seven. They were not happy about leaving our cozy northern neighborhood. That was the year Marilyn and I were offered the sitcom, and as much as I love baseball, it was hardly an opportunity we could turn down. Our husbands quit jobs that hey hated and we packed our bags and headed south to be on V. It sounds so hillbilly-like, doesn't it? "Gosh, Pa . . . look, hey have so many palm trees here!"

One of our first priorities after moving to L.A. was to get the kids settled. We got them signed up at Little League, knowing that the fun of families sharing this all-American pastime was the perfect remedy for our homesick boys. We all looked forward to opening day. We considered baseball the glue that holds entire countries together. It would be the glue that held us together. In a new city that was so unfamiliar we could count on a hokey parade and some local veterans to lead us into our first Little League season in L.A. Right? Well, sort of. . . .

We pulled into the parking lot, and other than the fact that it was lined with BMWs, Land Cruisers and Volvo station wagons, it was exactly what we expected. As we made our way to the field, we heard the announcer say that Melissa Manchester would be singing the National Anthem. We thought, "Oh, that is so funny, she has the same name as the famous *Midnight at the Oasis* Melissa!" As we approached the stands we saw a fuzzy redhead behind the microphone. It was Melissa Manchester! We were so impressed and even a little thankful that we didn't have to give patronizing applause to the off-key veterans this year. We climbed up into the bleachers as the "real" Steve Allen began his opening remarks. The field was flooded with the Warner Brothers characters—from Bugs Bunny to Yosemite Sam! Then Cybill Shepherd was invited to throw out the first ball! My husband turned to me and said, "We certainly are not in Kansas anymore!"

All four of us stood there in amazement as our new Little League's opening day unfolded. Bryce turned to me, glove in hand, and said, "Mommy, when's the parade?" There were no kids on bikes with tattered gloves, no licorice at the snack stand

and no hokey parade! It was like opening day at Dodger Stadium. What planet do these people live on? Don't they know that it's all about the free Sno-Kone? I had a coronary when someone suggested donating money to put misters in the dugouts to keep the kids cool all summer. Was this the Golden Door or was it Little League? Play ball!

Well, it has come to be that this is our life. After four years these people don't seem so famous anymore. Your value in Little League is based solely on how good your kid is at the game. In other words, it's actually much more brutal than Hollywood itself. This is the land of baseball controversy. There are more rules here than in election financing. We couldn't help suspecting that the parents who seem to take it all a little too seriously probably sucked at the sport themselves. These are the fathers who are getting injured themselves at practice. We watch grown men trying to hit infield warm-ups and swinging the bat so far around they fall down.

The fathers are generally much more into it than the mothers. Not that there aren't a whole group of over-the-top team moms who can give a candy sale the same importance as airlifting supplies into Bosnia.

As a rule, I tend to shy away from any man who comes to a Little League practice in a full major-league uniform with his own name embroidered on the back. If your kid gets on his team, you know it's going to be a long season. This is a man who is mixing up his fantasies and his real life. This is a man who has little children practicing five days a week. I wonder why these men aren't able to see it themselves, or, if they do, why they don't look into getting some help. Maybe baseball fantasy/therapy camp. I'm so thankful my husband got it out of his system early in his life and especially thankful that he doesn't have a uniform that still fits.

During our last season, there was a team that had lost eight of the nine games it had played, which had taken its toll on the kids and more so on the coach. He snapped in a most ugly manner. He sat the kids down in their dugout and proceeded to pace in front of them like a bull going in for the kill. Then, with all his pent-up steam and anger, nostrils flaring and neck veins popping, he began to curse these kids up and down. The parents stood there speechless, shocked and unable to respond. His wife knew how to defuse the situation. She jumped up on the chain-link fence and started yelling at her husband and said, "Honey, you're being an asshole . . . Honey, all the parents are talking about you . . . Honey, you're giving our family a really bad name." What she really wanted to say, but she held her tongue, was, "I can't believe I'm married to this jerk."

Now, I know this man, and he really is a nice guy in real life, for the most part. I couldn't believe the words coming out of his mouth, stuff I'd never even heard before. So now you have a coach in a full baseball uniform screaming at ten-year-olds . . . what a nice, relaxing, esteem-building Saturday afternoon!

To drive home the insanity of it all, there was actually a national news piece about our Little League during the divisional playoffs last year. There were Little League coaches, probably in full Dodger uniforms, digging through the trash of opposing teams' players looking for utility bills and receipts. They were trying to prove that these twelve-year-olds with the batting averages of Babe Ruth didn't live within the proper boundaries to play on the team they were losing to. Is this what it has come to? Don't people have jobs during the day? I don't have time to take out my own trash, much less dig through someone else's.

The kids themselves are the only ones who have it all in perspective. If only the weekend warrior fathers could follow their

lead. One year during the city championships there was a bo
on my husband's team who asked in the bottom of the sevent
inning, with the score tied at 6–6, when the game was going t
be over, because his grandma was taking him to McDonald'
after the game. My husband lifted the cap off his head
scratched himself and said, "Go ahead and go, Al." With a hug
smile, Al grabbed his glove and then his grandma's hand and
said, "I did good, huh, Grams?" That moment remains one o
my husband's fondest coaching memories. He said it really
made him see why he was out there all spring and summer—
for just plain fun. To expect more would be futile!

It's only fun, though, through May. Around June, frankly, I
begin to tire of the whole thing. The kids try out in February
and if you're lucky, the regular season ends in June. Then if you
are luckier still, your kid makes the All-Star team and that team
keeps winning. This year Eric played until July 12. Now, I
can't be the only killjoy out there, can I? Everyone was so
excited that the boys kept winning and I was, too . . . until
it started to eat away at my summer vacation and my gut. I had
been eating Bob's dugout dogs since February and I was getting
canker sores from the Skittles. I had permanent indentations in
my cellulite from the bleachers and I was having a hard time
concentrating on the game. With every victory, the mothers
would cheer and then exchange that "I can't believe we're still
winning" look.

My son was in the playoff game of the century and my husband was inches from wearing a full uniform himself, pacing
up and down the sidelines with tears in his eyes. Eric came up
to bat with two outs in their last inning at bat. Now, you'd think
a good mother would be hanging on to every tense moment. I
was trying, but it was 102 degrees in July and something else
had my attention. There had been a woman there during the

ntire All-Star journey who would sit in the bleachers with her iends, disclosing every personal tidbit about her entire life. I new her taste in men leaned toward the buff only, I knew she hopped at Bloomingdale's, wore the outfits and then took hem back, I even knew the name of her personal waxer and he shape she was waxed in in the bikini area. What I didn't now was the reason she'd had a little Band-Aid on the bottom of her chin for the last six weeks. Why had she not mentioned hat? What was under there? Through all that gossiping she never made reference to that Band-Aid! When Eric got up to bat, I was distracted—all I could think of was "This might be the end of the season and I still haven't found out what was under that Band-Aid." I was totally consumed and obsessed by it. I kept trying to come up with creative ways to knock it off. "Maybe if I spilled my Coke on her face the moisture would make it fall off." I'm not proud to show my immaturity here. I had to know . . . I wouldn't be able to sleep.

Well, our team hung on for another inning but eventually lost. There were hugs and tears and the closing of another chapter. Another season and summer gone and I still didn't know what was under that Band-Aid. I had to get brilliant, fast. On the way to our cars I pretended that I had cut myself and needed to borrow a Band-Aid. I had her! It wasn't like she could say no, she had to wave the one on her chin at me just to answer the question. She graciously said, "Sure, I have a whole box." She handed me one and drove off saying, "Congratulations, your son made a great play!" . . . What play?

So there I stood with a useless Band-Aid, having missed my own son's crowning moment, all in the name of my own kind of "Little League dementia." At least the father in the uniform saw the play. At least the coaches can focus. At least the men in the uniforms understand how fleeting these moments can be and maybe that's why they want it all to be so perfect. Mayb there's nothing wrong with wanting to do it over again wit your own kids, and maybe, if I promise to pay real good atter tion, I might be able to get a uniform in a woman's size larg and enough confidence to say, "Hey, babe . . . what the hell wa under that Band-Aid you wore all last year?"

Attitude or Gratitude

Caryl and I are "family first" people. We won't take just any job that pays well that takes us away from the family. When we do go away, we keep it to a minimum and their dads are with the kids when we're not. Don't we sound like perfect little moms? The truth is, it's been our good luck that most often we are called out of town at the exact moment our kids go into their obnoxious cycle. Isn't it weird how your own child can look really ugly to you? There are those moments when your four-year-old looks up at you with red Squeeze It stains gunked on his teeth, a mucus trail going from his nose to his

ear and a sour look on his face and you think to yourself, "Ho
did I make that?"

Being "The Mommies" in more ways than one, it was re
hard on us when we first started doing shows on the road. W
couldn't leave the kids for days at a time, even if they were i
great hands with their fathers, and not feel the guilty par
Guilt. Guilt. Guilt. We'd be weeping waifs in the airport when
ever we'd see another parent with her child. Everybody feel
terrible when we miss a Little League game or a dance recital
You'd have to be pretty removed not to feel the pang of guilt i
you missed the school play, but I wonder if men are pro-
grammed as much as women to feel guilty if they're not
around for the little things like homework or blow-drying their
daughter's hair for picture day. Guilt. Guilt. Guilt.

Leaving the kids in their father's care is especially hard on
the controlling mom. That would be me. I always think I
know what's best in every circumstance and I use my
maternal right to push my ideas on my kids until they will
no longer let me, around the time they turn seven. Kids have
fun when Dad's in charge. Kids eat neat stuff when Dad's in
charge. Kids dress differently when Dad's in charge. I would
leave Marcy in a cute little Gap Kids jumper with matching
tights and I'd come home to Pippi Longstocking. No matter
how much I organized ahead of time, they had their own way
of doing things.

Caryl and I were called out of town for five days when
Marcy was in kindergarten. I was already quite prepared for the
upcoming United Colors of Benetton Day, when each child had
to come to school representing a different country. I'd gone to
Chinatown in San Francisco the week before and selected a tiny
turquoise satin outfit for Marcy from Taiwan, cute little slippers

d all. On the day of the event I was in Texas. Richard, using hair gel and quite a selection of brushes and bobby pins, rigged up a most impressive chignon, in the shape of a vertical figure eight, right on the top of little Marcy's head. It was so tight it pulled Marcy's eyes into the shape needed to complete the outfit. Oh, were the other mothers impressed! I can't tell you how many times I heard about that glorious bun. I suspect they may have been a little jealous. Think about it, I had a husband who could whip up a chignon! The husband envy wore off when, encouraged by the attention he had received, Richard would re-create the "do" every single time I went out of town. I think he couldn't wait for me to leave. I'd catch him buying new accouterments and gel. Whenever I would phone

Marcy with her famous chignon.

home, poor little Marcy would whine to me that she had a headache.

These days it's hard to make ends meet, and I know ple[n] of working moms who would give anything to be a stay-[at] home mom.

One time we were booked in Las Vegas for a four-day r[un] that went through Halloween. We thought we made it clear [to] our agents that we wouldn't, *couldn't*, be away for trick-o[r] treating. No one paid attention. They sure were surprise[d] when we got on that plane. I was sewing Marcy's fairy costum[e] all the way home. I just couldn't bear the thought of the othe[r] kids running through the neighborhood with their moms clos[e] by and Marcy with an aching head from the bun and her absen[t] mom off telling jokes. Doesn't that sound pitiful?

It's not that I can't live without being near my children al[l] the time. Marcy went away to summer camp for two weeks this year and I was just fine. I wasn't the one leaving, so I car- ried no guilt.

M   Guilt is the culprit. Guilt. Guilt. Guilt. Why do we feel so bad if we're not there with the kids for it *all*? I don't know about you, but one fear that bothers me is the image of my kids telling a future therapist that everything wrong in their lives was my fault. This fear is stupid because they'll end up on that same couch anyway; might as well give them something to talk about.

Caryl and I had to go to New York for four days recently and as usual, I called home every night. There is a routine we do on the phone: (1) Check in with Rich, ask how it's going (this goes by quickly . . . he's a man of few words). (2) Ask Marcy how it's going and she always replies, "Good," followed by complaints about something in school, then we do a little homework. (3) A quick notice of bribery on my part: "I got you a cool pre- sent . . ." (4) Time for good-byes and love-yous to both.

This particular time, Marcy was completing a writing

signment entitled "How I Became President" while I was in
ew York. The concept being that nobody does it alone, not
ven the President. We talked about teamwork and I told her
o think about the people who gave her the most support. I
ouldn't wait to see what she had written. I just knew she would
nmortalize me; after all, I was a "family first" kind of mom.

As soon as I got home, she proudly read me her essay. She
xplained how pleased she was to be president and that she had
o many people to thank. Somewhere near the middle she
wrote, "My dad helped me by teaching me how to give good
speeches. My mom was gone a lot pursuing her acting career."
What?!? Well, stab me in the heart with a big ol' knife and twist
that sucker!

"Acting career?? Acting career? Is that what you think I'm
doing? Well, let me set the record straight, missy!" My hurt feelings quickly turned into anger. "I never once left your side until
you were seven years old. And even on those few nights, I made
sure you were with family, never with a baby-sitter. I nursed
your little butt, I brought you everywhere I went, I had an epi-
siotomy for you!" Then I became lost in the whole concept.
"President? You think I was too damn busy to help you become
president? Who helped with your homework? Who made sure
you got a good education? Who taught you how to dress for
success? Who! You wouldn't even *be* president if I hadn't mod-
eled how women can take charge of their own lives! You
wouldn't have even thought about *running* for president if it
weren't for me!!"

"Mom," Marcy began in a timid voice, "I'm *not* the president . . . it was only a class assignment." Then she added, "I'm
sorry."

Gratitude. When does the gratitude start? Was I that blind
to my mother's efforts at being there for me? I think maybe I

was. I guess as kids we just expect our moms to be there for us. We don't know about the effort. Gratitude comes easier now that I'm an adult and see how hard it is.

My high school graduation present was a trip to Disneyland for a week with some friends. Mom stayed up all night the night before, making new summer dresses for me to wear on my trip. I think now of the love and effort she always made to give me a lot of wardrobe choices. She sewed everything, but ingrate me wanted store-bought clothes. What I wouldn't give now for some of that intricate craftsmanship she put into her work. When she first noticed that I *forgot* the new dresses she had just made, was she as angry as I was about Marcy's papers? Or was she sad, thinking her daughter didn't care? I was just a clueless teenager on my first trip to Disneyland. I didn't think about being grateful.

M I'm grateful for teachers. My God, have you ever volunteered in the classroom? They are saints. If it weren't for teachers, Mother's Day would be a bust, don't you think? I would never get the gifts that meant the most to me: the little ceramic handprints, the macaroni necklaces. Hell, on Mother's Day, the wife is usually the one orchestrating the gift giving anyway. She's the one that stresses about getting her mother and her husband's mother something nice. The best present I could ever get for Mother's Day would be a list from my kids of things they remember I did to show them love, accompanied by photos, music and possibly poetry. Am I asking too much of them?

Sometimes my husband puts me in a position of "grateful but irritated." One birthday he very kindly asked me what I wanted. I told him that I wanted to have the antique wristwatch that belonged to my mother repaired so I could use it. I told him of its sentimental value and how it would make me ppy if someone else made the effort to get it fixed. That's ally the only gift I could think of. I didn't really need a new atch, but I just loved my mother's old watch.

Come my birthday he handed me a small gift box just large nough to hold a wristwatch. I smiled at him tenderheartedly vhile I opened it. As I lifted the top of the case, Richard said oftly, "I hope you like it."

Yes, there was a watch in that box, but it was a brand-new Timex. I hate those moments. There's just no time to prepare. Your head is saying, "What the hell is THIS?" while your mouth is saying, "Oh, honey, thank you." Your face is contorting as you push out thoughts like "Did he hear NOTHING?"

I put the watch on with disdain, sporting a forced smile. Still, he was so sweet. He meant well. And a gift is a gift. I never did get that antique watch repaired and he never knew of my disappointment. I found a way to be grateful for a Timex.

My neighbor Joanne tells me of a thoughtful and romantic anniversary present that actually got her mad. Was it attitude or lack of gratitude, or neither? You decide.

Joanne had her eye on a new dining room set for about a year. She's the one who pays the bills in their family and she had been carefully paying off the credit card and budgeting for about nine months for the new furniture. Every day Joanne would visualize how nice her house would look with new dining room furniture. (We women get fixated on things like that.) Disappointed that she couldn't serve their anniversary dinner on the new set, she figured she still had about two more months of scrimping to go.

After they dined on roast leg of lamb and sipped on some Merlot, Ed proudly handed her a small velvet jewelry box containing a beautiful anniversary diamond ring. It was so exquisite it took Joanne's breath away. She looked up at her husband

of fifteen years and slowly asked, "Ed, where did you get th
money for this ring?" To which he replied enthusiastically, "O!
I put it on the credit card." She pictured herself writing th
check for the diamond ring each month on her old dining roor
set for the next five years. "Ed, I want you to take it back."

"Joanne! I can't take it back."

"Yes, you can."

"But it's beautiful and you deserve a nice ring."

"No, Ed. I deserve a nice dining room set!"

"Huh?"

And what began as a romantic evening of celebration ended
up as a regular husband-wife quarrel. The fight didn't last too
long, though. Ed returned the ring the next day, and the clerk
was horrified that his wife had made him take it back. She commented that it was such a generous gift and questioned why his
wife wasn't more grateful. Ed said something about not being
able to eat off the ring.

Two months later they were entertaining some guests. The
table was set nicely and when asked if it was new, Joanne said,
"Yes, it's an anniversary gift from Ed."

O. Henry would be so proud.

Quality Time and Special Days

*E*very time I turn around there is something else in the news that makes me feel as if I'm not a very good parent. There's always some other thing that I didn't know I should have done, either in utero or out of the utero. We are always finding new and inventive ways to feel guilty or less than good at the job we're doing as parents. The area where I feel the most vulnerable is the area of "quality time." I know what it is and I know it when I see it, but most of the time I am with my children there is nothing quality about it. Trying to plan for quality is even worse! That has always, clearly, been a recipe for disaster. It seems as though every time I make an attempt at

planning "the perfect day" for my children, it backfires. Usual
we aren't even out of the driveway before the battle for th
front seat begins in earnest. Having stopped myself at breedin
only two children, I have now worked it out that one gets th
front seat on odd days, the other one on even days. Before yo
think I'm really clever, I want you to know that it took me te
years to figure that out and it's about *all* I have worked out. I
is the nature of children to nag each other. They could care les
about the effort you have put into planning the "special day" o
bonding. They have us so under control. They know we wil
threaten and coerce and scream at them to be nice to each
other. They also know we will do it all again in about a month
or so because we must soothe our souls with the notion, if not
the reality, of quality time.

    I believe that one of the biggest requirements of being a
"good" parent is seeing to it that their little lives are taken
care of through appointments. In fact, how well your
parental performance is has a direct correlation with how
many appointments you have scheduled that week. One eye
exam appointment equals one parental bonus point. One eye
exam and a teeth cleaning, two parental bonus points. Now,
with the increasing onslaught of those damned newsmagazine
shows, the expectation is changing and out of control. This
past year I must have been especially sensitive about what I
"should" be doing to turn my children into healthy, politically
correct, sensitive and intelligent adults, because I started keeping track of every little study that appeared in the news. It's no
wonder we're all feeling bombarded. This is the laundry list of
the things society actually believes we should be doing, this
year anyway, for our children and ourselves, every single day.
This is in addition to your run-of-the-mill dental appointments
and haircuts and so on. All this in order to sleep guilt-free.

.   Read to your children twenty minutes a day to increase their vocabulary.

2. Do thirty minutes of meditation to be a more relaxed and better parent.

3. Floss your and your children's teeth twice a day so they have healthy teeth as adults.

4. Limit their television watching to one hour. There is a direct correlation between the amount they watch and their success in school.

5. Get your kids off the couch and exercising or they'll be couch potato adults.

6. Drink plenty of water and encourage your kids to do it, it's just a good habit.

7. Use cloth diapers and any other nondisposable plastics— our landfills are maxed out.

8. Be a room parent or volunteer at school and your kids will imitate you and be more community-oriented.

9. Teach them responsibility by giving them chores to do every day. It will make them independent.

10. Feed your kids four servings of vegetables. They are brain food.

11. Give them vitamin C. Studies are still showing that kids who take it are healthier and get sick less often.

12. Use at least a level 15 sunscreen on you and your kids every day to prevent melanoma.

These "shoulds" are hard for someone like myself. I've always been one to choose spontaneity over health. Unfortu-

nately, it doesn't help with the guilt. I also believe that if I cou
do half of what's recommended on a semiregular basis, I a
my kids would be the most anal and boring people to l
around. People who are strict about the choices they make f
their children tend not to be my friends. I like to surrour
myself with others who cheat, and encourage my cheatin₃
Besides, if we really do all these things, just plain *living* hasn
left any room for quality time. I just didn't think I would hav
to be so attentive as a mother. It's a good thing I wasn't payin₃
attention to these studies before I got pregnant. What grea
birth control!

I know that our parents didn't spend one-hundredth of the
time thinking about our well-being as we do about our chil
dren's. My theory is that none of us would have to if we didn't
always have to compare ourselves to that perfect little coordinated "ideal" of a nineties woman. How do these women
do it all so gracefully? They always seem to have a short,
curt name like "Barb." The name Barb just screams color-
coordinated, doesn't it? Well, as I see it, everything was fine
until "Barb" started flaunting her organized little self all up and
down the neighborhood and on TV. She drives a minivan that
has no Cheerios smashed into the backseat. Apparently her
kids eat breakfast at the table. Her hair is always perfectly in
place, with a matching headband. She always appears to have
time to do all those extra things, like put love notes in their
lunch bags. Her children are dressed perfectly, too. Their Gap
outfits are always stain-free and their noses never run. She is
the mom who actually remembers the bottled water for her
son on soccer day. She is the mom who actually brings home-
baked cookies on doilies to the class party. During every holiday their house is decorated, symmetrically. In fact, she was
probably the one who invented the banners I'm starting to see

rywhere. Tell me, where do people store that crap? I sup-
se in neatly organized and labeled containers. She is the
m the rest of us love to hate, through no fault of her own.
s simply because she makes the rest of us all feel so inferior.

We have an over-the-top Barb on our street. There have
en been times when I've actually seen her outside playing
.I. Joe with her kids. Now, I'm sorry, I'm all for spending time
ith your kids, but I think Barb probably has a little army fetish
at needs to be exposed. Any grown woman willing to play
oot-'em-up outside in fatigues doesn't have a life. I may
nore my children's pleas for me to play with them, but really,
think her kids' therapy bills will be enormous later on. At
ast, that's what I tell myself. Moms like Barb have got to be
n speed.

There has to be some kind of credit given to those of us
who are well-meaning but just let it go. Keeping up with the
oneses or the Barb Joneses has become an impossible standard.
Especially in light of the fact that almost everything will give us
cancer or kill us anyway. Even if we did it all perfectly, that bac-
terium from the chicken, that is now in the sponge, which is
now on the knife, that is now in the cutting board, is going to
make us all sick. So really, what's the point? So I groom my children to a tee, follow them around with Kleenex and bring
cookies on the doily to the class party. That isn't going to matter much when we discover that our house was built within
two hundred yards of an electric tower that has been emitting
unhealthy levels of radioactivity since my husband and I had
the romp that conceived them. No wonder there's apathy. I live
for the day when Barb discovers that the four servings of vegetables she's been feeding those little darlings have enough pes-
ticide on them to eradicate the entire medfly community.
Knowing her, she'll probably just suit up the family in color-

coordinated Agent Orange helmets on their way to the library to study about Chernobyl.

Deep down, I know what it means to be a good mom. I also know that there is a whole group of parents who get off on complaining about how bad they are as parents, I don't mean to be that parent. There is so much to be said for just purging all of it. It's the parents who are trying to hold it all together whose kids we know will end up as criminals. It is the maintaining of the facade that is so exhausting for all of us. I think it is better for the parents of those out-of-control kids just to make the disclaimer "Look, we worked a lot last year and now we have some behavioral things to work on."

I used to berate my own mother for caring so much about what other people thought, and here I am now doing the same. My mother would have gotten so much mileage out of just admitting to the fact that she cared what other people thought. Let's face it. We judge everyone around us by the actions of their kids. In general, loser kid, loser parents. That is, until your kid's the loser. For those parents who obviously haven't had enough quality time, if they would just admit it, they would all earn extra parental bonus points.

When it comes down to it, I think quality time comes in very small and unexpected increments. It is nothing we can plan or manipulate. Generally it costs no money and rewards you immensely. They are the moments that creep up on you, like walking by your children's room and finding the two suburban commandos, who twenty seconds before almost bludgeoned each other to death, in a sweet brotherly embrace. It is the nights when we find ourselves playing a silly game of chase around the island in the kitchen, laughing hysterically because everyone happened to be in a good mood when some smartass comment was made about my cooking. It's

looking down on a family that is stressed out and trying to
it *all* right *all* the time and saying, "Wake up, it's right in
ont of you."

Caryl's boys in matching sweaters. The only time
she managed a Barb-style threesome.

The Language of Families

There are many things that serve as the glue that bonds the family together. Family traditions, religious beliefs, ethnic backgrounds, sometimes a common enemy will hold a family tight, then there's the diminishing, but important, frequent family meal and one of my favorites: family language.

It usually begins when we are in the early stages of coupling. It's as if we're trying out the process of naming baby, only "baby" is usually male genitalia, Peter being the standard.

his also is the period of time when the pet name emerges. ven the most stoic, manly man will become "Cupcake." chard used to call me his "tender." I suppose I'm "well done" w. When I was married to Larry, he was Led and I was Med. me of my old friends still call me that.

When my little brother, Paul, was trying to say "horse" he alled it a yo and it's been yo to me for going on thirty-five ears now. I've spread yo to other friends in other states, too. Hmmmm. I wonder if the rappers are actually saying, "Horse, aby! Waz up?" You never know.

When the boys were teens we had a family shorthand that ust irritated them. A conversation might go like this: "Richie, better get some Foo Foo Juice [aftershave] because a couple of Oh La Las [girls] called and said they'd be over soon."

Taun Taun is a nickname we have for Marcy, but it has evolved to be applied when a person does something very naughty, but they are so cute they get away with it. It has everything to do with attitude. For example, Tammy Faye is a Taun Taun, Paula Jones is not. Goldie Hawn could easily be a Taun Taun, Courtney Love could not. Rosie O'Donnell is a Taun Taun, Barbara Walters is not. Danny DeVito is, Al Pacino is not. You get the idea. Who in your life is a Taun Taun?

*C*onfusion over the English language doesn't ever end, no matter how old we become. Something always needs translating, explaining and sometimes removal. Bryce once came home after playing at a friend's house and asked me Dick was a dirty word or his uncle's name. He said that h friend Mark told him it was a dirty word and he better stop sa ing it. "Well, honey, Dick is my brother's name and it is also dirty word. Dick was a name first, I think, but then, when became slang for penis, it took on a whole new meaning an that's why your Aunt Anne won't let us call him anything bu Richard now." He tossed me that puzzled puppy look. I ha given him far too much information for a simple little question

Words are such funny things. Growing up as one of eleve children, we developed a code or secret language within ou four walls. There were shortcuts and abbreviations that made conversations quicker or less embarrassing or just more fun My favorite thing at dinnertime when I was little was when my dad would play the "Sagers" game. Sagers was an imaginary bogeyman my father invented. He would knock with one hand under the table pretending to be Sagers, and if we didn't finish our dinners Sager was going to come and grease our ears and swallow us whole. Not a very pleasant thing to tell young children, but I loved it. When our friends came over they were afraid of Sagers. We only found out because Dickey Rauch came over for dinner and was afraid to say no every time my dad offered him more food. He went home and vomited for hours. His mother suspiciously asked, "Who's Sagers?"

My father's name is Robert, but he goes by the familiar "Bob," which by the way is Bob spelled backward. Bob, as it turns out, is a nice short name for just about anything. My dad was always the fix-it guy, but when Dad fixed something, it was always done in the most efficient way with whatever was left over around the house. God forbid he should go to the hardware store for the actual part needed to do it correctly. For example, if a picture on the wall kept getting bumped, causing it to hang askew, then "Bob" would simply drive a molly bolt right through the outside of the frame. How lovely! Mom would come running in, always just late enough to prevent the destruction.

My dad loves a good roaring fire—he was raised in the East. In southern California we rarely have reason to build one, but when my dad was in the mood, stand back, because anything in proximity became firewood. I've never seen my mother so upset as the night my dad burned an old beat-up wooden rocker that unfortunately was an antique that her best friend had loaned her years ago. She had never gotten around to returning it and now it was keeping us warm on a chilly eighty-degree evening.

At Christmastime you could always count on my dad to attach a large cable to the Christmas tree to keep it upright. Not very attractive, but there was more surface to hang lights on! It was like living on a cruise ship where everything was bolted down. So in his honor, to this day, if anyone accomplishes a task in a less than tidy way, it is simply called "Bobing it." Sorry, Dad.

We also had a dog when I was growing up that we called Hercules for his mythic ability to drag things twice his size. When Hercules came bounding into a room we'd sing, "Hercules Puppy Pud, here to save the day!" Puppy Pud? What is that? I still don't know and I still use it with my own dogs.

Sometimes families invent words for things because they don't want to use the technical or clinical word for it. *Vagina* falls into that category a lot. My best friend, Martha, Dickie's older sister, taught me that their family called it a "puddy." Close to "Puppy Pud" in name, not meaning. Other friends of ours called it the "Chooch," which sort of sounds like what it is. When I started asking people what their special family word for "it" was, they shared all sorts of bizarre nicknames with equally funny explanations, such as "ginee goat" and "China." My husband has taught our children to call the general region, for either men or women, "The Box Office." In fact, my husband is the king of code words. When I get my period, the code words are . . . that I have "Blue Dog." In my mother's day they called it "falling off the roof," maybe because that's how you felt. Len calls sleeping over at someone's house, when sex is involved, having an "Away Game." Sex is called "Verta Verta Whoah Whoah" . . . that's a lot of words for something as simple as sex. He calls fat "adipose"—that one is left over from the only thing he remembers from biology. In fact I would venture to say that amusing our family with the English language is one of my husband's greatest gifts.

Twisted Parenting

Bribery Gets You Everywhere

*T*here is no way to teach a child how to use the potty. He must be bribed to use the potty. There is absolutely no reason why a child would want to stop playing G.I. Joes or Polly Pockets long enough to go to the bathroom. This is admittedly the low road of parenting, but in the end we just want to move that little butt to the toilet, right? This is also about the only time when the materialism of the world we live in actually works to our benefit. I say . . . use it!

I was your typical mother worried about the fact that at three years old Bryce had developed an obsession with army anything. I was embarrassed that he fantasized about shooting

things and killing things and blowing heads off of things a
such a young age. I hid from people the fact that my son slep
with a sword. I certainly was embarrassed the Christmas that
smuggled the G.I. Joe Command Center past the war toy pick
eters at Toys "R" Us. I tried to steer him toward animals and
nature and art, but he really just wanted to blow them up, too.
I finally gave in and went with the "everything in moderation"
credo. In the course of a year, we owned more equipment than
General Schwarzkopf. From the age of two to three years this
actually worked to my advantage by keeping him very enter-
tained. Then it came time for Bryce to go to preschool. First he
had to pass the entrance test, which is taken on a toilet. You
don't hit the rim, you don't get in. We had to get this child
potty-trained. He was three and I had a brand-new two-month-
old draining the lifeblood out of me at night.

This was not an easy task. I was so eager and excited
that the first time he made it to the bathroom twice in a
row, I figured he was potty-trained. I called and signed
him up for preschool . . . albeit a little prematurely. The
thought of a morning with a couple hours of freedom made
me warm with excitement. I loaded up on Batman, G.I. Joe and
Thundercat underwear. Action Pants was what they were
called. I was in denial as to exactly how much "action" those
pants would really see.

I dropped him off and sped home to put the baby down for
a nap, and if I was lucky, a cup of coffee in silence. It was but a
moment of ecstasy. About an hour later, the preschool called
and said, "Come and get him, he's not potty-trained."

I begged and pleaded and swore it was just a little regression
he was experiencing. Having heard the desperation in my
voice, they let him stay. This went on every day for about three

days. Like clockwork, they would call, I would plead, and I would pick him up holding his underwear in a Ziploc baggie. The director of the school gently pulled me aside and explained that my son had to go and he couldn't come back until he could hold it. Potty-training Bryce became my obsession. It had now become all-consuming. Bryce sensed our urgency, he smelled blood and as a result had more setbacks than ever before.

On our restocking trips to Toys "R" Us, we would buy one potty-training manual with every G.I. Joe or Sergeant Slaughter. We tried every new approach that promised to encourage and reward the most basic of human instincts.

We did the "positive reinforcement" technique and that didn't work. We did the "run them to the potty after every meal timetable" and that didn't work. We did the "all the family pile in and go to the bathroom together," and that failed, too. Then we said, "Screw it. You want those G.I. Joes so bad, Bryce . . . you are gonna have to work for 'em." So I took the brand-new Sergeant Slaughter and put it back in the packaging all nice and pretty. Then I manipulatively displayed it above the TV set in full view of my little trooper. He screamed for his guy. Through sobs and hysteria you could hear "Guy . . . Guy . . . Guy," which sounded an awfully lot like "Die . . . Die . . . Die! I chose to hear the former. The method was so simple. You pee, you play. Every time Bryce successfully made it to the toilet, he could keep the G.I. Joe in his possession. When he chose to walk around with poop in his pants, leaving bunny bullets in his path, the "guy" went back into the packaging on top of the television. Within two days we had completed our mission.

Every child psychologist would warn against the wrong reason for motivating the behavior and so on. And to those health professionals, I simply say, "He is now fourteen, he doesn't play with guns and he is still making it to the bathroom." As the years have gone by, I have employed that method successfully many times.

If only he'd still settle for a G.I. Joe.

The Education Of My Little Trees

There's nothing like a first-time mother in the school system. We are zealots. We can turn a principal into butter with our enthusiasm and give him the biggest bunch of hard-working ulcers the very next day. We can manipulate a child's grade with one good fund-raiser. Watch out, because Mother Bear is here to make sure no one's messing with her little one.

The fierce protection lessens with each child. I remember sitting at a preschool meeting for Marcy and listening to mothers complain that the children didn't get enough outings where they could learn how best to serve their community. One mother wanted a group of four-year-olds to go to public parks for the sole purpose of picking up litter. Another was on t[...] usual no-sugar tirade. I sat back with amusement as I thoug[...] of my teenage boys driving around eating Twinkies and tos[...] ing the wrappers. Yeah, I taught them about those things whe[...] they were little, too.

Once my kids were in grammar school, Richie, the oldes[...] was the easiest one. I didn't have to fight any battles in hi[...] honor. He had strong work ethics straight from the begin[...] ning of preschool. He understood assignments, did his home[...] work, completed projects and took tests with the maturity o[...] a second-year grad student.

Aaron, on the other hand, was elusive. We got our first hin[...] of the future at his first-grade Open House. Clean and dressec[...] appropriately, Richard, Aaron and I excitedly entered the class[...] room. Each child's name was colorfully decorated and Scotch[...] taped to the front of his desk. We had a little trouble find- ing Aaron's, so we asked him to show us where he sat.

Beaming, he pointed to the only one up against the wall, separated from all the others, and announced, "I get to sit up here!"

"Could it be possible he had been in trouble?" I wondered as my eyes darted around the classroom to see if any other child's desk was flat against a wall.

"Look, Mommy! Look! There's my name!" He beamed and then pointed to the only name on the blackboard with four checks after it.

Richard and I shared a quick glance. Four checks? Carefully I asked, "Honey, what happens if you get five checks?"

He proudly blurted, "Oh, then I get to visit the principal!"

I could feel other parents' eyes on the back of my head. Through a pasted-on smile, I leaned next to my husband, low- ered my voice and said, *"He doesn't get it."*

Teachers usually had experienced his older brother in their class the year before. With Richie as their student, they would settle in as if someone had just handed them a big, warm blanket, then we'd rip the blanket right off, hit them with Aaron and give them a cold shower. Every year Back to School Night was the same. The first year the teacher would sing the praises of our star student who did schoolwork with passion. No doubt about it, Richie had drive. They'd compliment us on what a good job we were doing. The following year we'd walk into the classroom and that same glowing teacher would scowl at us. Wearing that "Where did you go wrong?" look, they would ask us to stay after the other parents had gone. Not only was Aaron adept at slithering out of work, but he was popular and others liked to imitate him. Icy-cold shower. We'd all agree to work on the problem, though none of us had a clue as to what to do. As always, just before we left, the teacher would ask in a rather longing voice, "How's Richie?" This scenario played itself out many times.

Aaron went to high school for five years. We never really knew what grade he was in. He was the kind of kid who would get an F in English and a C in Spanish. Whenever I went to his high school's Back to School Night, I would more often be one of two parents in the classroom. The majority of parents were over in the Honors Program section. I always felt compelled to give each teacher my disclaimer. I'd say that Aaron came from a loving, supportive home where we had no idea how to make him work, but we'd try.

In his senior year I was going to the *last* Back to School Night of Aaron's education. I was growing weary of all the English teachers that night. You see, his schedule contained Freshman, Sophomore, Junior *and* Senior English in order for him to graduate. Each classroom had been the same old story: "Aaron is a strong, evocative underachiever."

I entered his fifth period class, which was Forestry, and his teacher, Mr. Furrer, greeted me and asked about Richie. He also asked me to wait a minute after class. I knew the drill. After the other parents had filed out, he said, "Your son is so brilliant. It's such a joy to have him in the class."

I said in a rote manner, "Thanks, he's at Sacramento State now, majoring in environmental science and minoring in business administration."

Mr. Furrer looked at me quizzically. "I'm talking about Aaron."

I didn't move a muscle. My only thought was, "Am I in a dream?"

He went on: "He's clever and respectful. He participates in class discussions and is a leader. He's the first kid in four years to get an A on this particular test. He's so full of energy, he really lights up the room."

M I couldn't believe my ears. See, *I* think of him as lighting up a room. *I* see his brilliance. I had been waiting such a long time for someone else to notice it, I had given up. Tears began to well up.

Then he said, "Oh, and one more thing, he really loves you. And he's very proud of you. He talks to me about you a lot." I just stood there and cried. I was so touched that this kind-hearted teacher took the time to tell me.

I skipped sixth period and went straight to Caryl's. I walked in sobbing. She put her arm around me and asked, "Did it go badly?"

Through tears I said, "No."

"Then what's the matter?"

"A teacher likes him!"

Caryl started laughing, then, after a while, I joined her.

By the time Marcy was in school, I was well into my self-

lp phase. I had completed so many audiotapes, I was getting
oficient at taking responsibility for my own actions, having
e courage to say no, accepting the things I could not change
ad turning anything into a win-win situation. I thought we
ould start little Marcy in a Montessori program. I felt that the
espectful ways the teachers work with the children fit the bill.

One day I picked Marcy up from kindergarten and was
reeted by a tearful daughter. "What's the matter, hon?"

"I gave Emily an *I–Message* and she wouldn't say, 'I hear
ou.' Can I beat her up?"

Hey, she was only five. She hadn't yet read Wayne Dyer.

Marcy was in second grade when we moved to L.A., and we
tried to find a school compatible with what she was used to.
After much research, she ended up going to The Rainbow
Bridge.

The school had monthly meetings to educate new parents
in the philosophy of The Rainbow Bridge. Seems "the bridge"
was an intricate component. I came prepared with pen and
tablet in hand to find out all I could about this New Age philosophy. They lost me a little when two teachers carried on an
hour-long discussion regarding the meaning of "Rumpelstilts-
kin" and how it compares with today's society.

We formed a circle and another teacher took us foolishly
through a folk song and dance that our children were in the
process of learning. It's so unsightly to see big, old, self-conscious
adults leaping around a kids' classroom, don't you think? The
only thing worse is seeing big, old, *enthusiastic* adults leaping
around a kids' classroom.

They then had a question-and-answer period. One woman
told of this heartbreaking problem she was having. Her husband had passed away two years before and her five-year-old
daughter was asking when she could have him over for dinner.

The mother wanted to know how the school would hand such a problem. One teacher said it was best to answer h daughter *realistically*. I was completely agreeing until she we on to say that this woman should tell her little daughter to tr to remember when she was a baby in Heaven and finally got t choose her parents. How she came to Earth by way of Th Rainbow Bridge.

This teacher recommended that she tell her five-year-ol that her father had crossed back over The Rainbow Bridge Everyone was nodding in agreement. I could bear it no longer

I blurted out sarcastically, "Oh yeah, THAT'S very real!" I wa so irritated. I knew I had blasphemed. Everyone shot me a look then glanced at one another as if to say, "Guess we won't be seeing *her* on the other side of The Rainbow Bridge." Guess not.

All second-grade parents received an esoteric letter that same month from another parent whose daughter was in Marcy's class telling us her life story. She had been a victim in a bad marriage until the dolphins taught her to stand up for herself, and that's exactly what she intended to teach her daughter to do against the bullies of the school. I thought she meant she learned to be assertive from the Miami Dolphins, but was corrected by another parent. This school was annoying me.

Marcy learned many useful things at The Rainbow Bridge School: how to knit, how to yell at children in German and how to dance with the flow of nature.

We gave it a generous year and a half before we started looking elsewhere. Enough with the knitting, it was time to go back to basics. That is not an easy task in L.A. There are a few public schools that provide a safe and calm learning environment with lots of parental participation. Unfortunately, we didn't live near any of them. So college-prep private school it was.

In order to get accepted into most private schools in L.A., you and your child have to pass a series of tests. We had narrowed our choices down to two schools. The first one required a written test and separate child and parental interviews.

While Marcy was in the multipurpose room taking her written essay, fifteen sets of parents were listening to the principal explain that there were only two openings. She told us that they selected their students not only by their reading, writing, punctuation, syntax and math abilities, but most important, by what they had to say. Nowhere did I hear the words "knitting ability." She elaborated: "For example, your children right now are completing the writing assignment, Describe Your Favorite Day. Last year one little boy wrote that his favorite day was a time he spent fishing with his grandfather. He said that it did not matter if he caught a fish or didn't, that the time with his grandpa was what made the day good." The room "Awwwwww"-ed. She continued, "Sure, he had more than a few misspelled words. His penmanship needed a little work, too. Much more important, the fact that this young boy thought to write about his relationship with his grandfather touched our hearts. That's the kind of student we want here at Oak Hall." We all sighed.

What would Marcy write? I hoped she was writing about the time we brought clothes and toys to the battered women's shelter.

When the test was over, she came running to my arms. I asked her what she wrote as her favorite day. She replied excitedly, "I said that Christmas was my favorite day because I get lots of presents."

We applied at the other school. Their entrance test was far less stringent. This school was a perfect fit and it has been a great experience. She's in sixth grade now. I can't believe my youngest is almost finished with her elementary education. From the time my oldest was in preschool until now, I've been involved in the school system either as a parent, an art teacher, a drama coach, a PTO member, a teacher's aide or a room mother for the last *twenty* years. I wonder if when she's away at college, I'll get lonesome for one more Back to School Night.

Let's Talk About Sex, Baby . . .

Let's Talk About Sex, Uh-Huh . . .

*T*hose of us who grew up in the sixties and seventies now have children, and most of us pride ourselves on the fact that we are very open about sex with our children. We crow about starting to tell them about making love in both clinical and romantic terms. It's easy . . . as they grow and ask, we show and tell. Simple, right? Well, the part that we have all failed to realize is that maybe, just maybe, a fourteen-year-old pubescent boy doesn't want to hear about sex from his mother or father. It was fine at five, he adored me. At ten we giggled about it together. At fourteen there is absolutely nothing

redeeming about a sex talk with your parents. It's gross
matter what era you grow up in.

We have all said thousands of times that the thought of o
parents in a mad passionate embrace yelling, "Do me, baby, c
oh, do me!" is disgusting. Why, then, do we have blocka
when it comes to our own children? Do we honestly belie
that our fat will jiggle less, that our groaning and moaning
somehow more palatable than our own parents'? Most of
are riding around with a good twenty more pounds than ou
parents had at this age.

Why do we insist on burdening our children with our oper
ness? I learned about sex from Susie Vigas in the fifth grade
Now, as much as I chastise my parents for their lack of open
ness about sex, deep down I think I preferred it that way. Whe
I was in the fifth grade Susie was going to the public school
where they actually had a film and diagrams and stuff.
was a Catholic. We didn't get the talk until seventh grade,
long after most of the girls had already gotten their periods. A Catholic obstetrician, who used the altar as a stage and
had trouble pronouncing the word "menstruation," gave the lesson. He brought an easel with big cardboard diagrams that had
been poorly photocopied in eight-by-ten sections and then put
together like a puzzle. That was some uterus! The tension in that
church was as thick as a maxi pad with wings. Hearing about sex
with the Virgin Mary praying above you was not easy or enjoy-
able. Not that I didn't know a few girls who were hoping that the
immaculate conception thing might happen twice. I was so glad
that Susie had already filled me in. It's good to feel superior
when it comes to sex. That's something I've always carried with
me. We had cookies and punch afterwards. I was so happy to get
the hell out of there and tell Susie all about it. At least she had
told me how it was done the right way. So I thought.

Susie came home that day from fifth grade bursting with the energy that someone has when they carry a fabulous secret. The two of us ran behind her house to a secret place where she proceeded to draw in the dirt, with a stick, the biggest, scariest penis I have ever seen! "This can't be true, I will never let something like that near me. . . . And pubic hair, oh no, I don't even *want* pubic hair . . ." Susie and I mulled this information over and over and over. We talked about it well into that summer. Eventually we just grew up and got pubic hair and periods. We forget a lot of things from our childhood, but none of us ever forget the first time we hear about sex.

Fast-forward to today. We don't need sticks and a pile of dirt to teach our children. We have teaching aids. We leave nothing to the imagination. We have videos and books and some of us even have models. Big rubber uteruses are being pulled out of teachers' drawers all across America. Our imaginations were scary enough. Now our children are forced to confront the actual unfair size of the birth canal. Pubic hair is actually being displayed as if it was Jose Eber's secret hair. Last year at my kids' school one of the earth mothers insisted on making the gingerbread men and women with full genitalia, out of icing. Nobody blinked. Hansel and Gretel with green coconut pubic hair and yellow nipples! "Please, give me back my praying Virgin Mary!"

So we teach our kids all the right terms and we make an attempt to explain the process, but let's face it, we all know that until you actually do the deed, it's a hard thing to really understand. "Oh, so that's an erection! Wow, it's not as bad as the picture and it works so much better than the model!" It takes many years for our minds to put all the pieces of the puzzle together.

They say that kids are sponges only for what they are ready

to understand at that particular developmental age. For instance, my youngest son could not hold on to the proper pronunciation of the word "vagina" until he was about nine. Maybe because to him the vagina wasn't something he needed to know to play Super Mario Brothers 3. For years he called it a *BA-gina,* another addition to our family language. We laughed and repeated it until in our house it became known as the ba-gina. Years went by and we never thought to correct him. Which was fine as long as he kept it in the house. Unfortunately, it is part of the "Children's Union" to expose the public to anything your family would find embarrassing. When his school started teaching a human development class, we thought, "Great! They do the hard part and we come in for cleanup." What we didn't realize was that our confident, open child would spend an entire class time debating "vagina" and "ba-gina" with the teacher. The parent-teacher conference didn't go so well that year.

Then for a long time it seemed as if we were all on the same page about sexual facts. When it came up in movies, we discussed our values and it was comfortable again. Then it happened. We were on vacation. With all four of us staying in a small hotel room, the quarters were cramped. There was one bathroom. Early one morning I was putting on my makeup in the bathroom when my groggy, half-asleep son came in to do morning target practice. As I glanced down I looked in horror at what had become of my sweet, innocent young son. What had happened to him was shocking. Where had I been? He was huge! He had pubic hair! He was a man and he hadn't even bothered to let me in on it! And to think that I had put Desitin on his little butt rash only a year ago. What a year it had been. My little boy had been replaced by a very pubescent stranger. He had an entire package in place and ready to go. In shock, yet

ing to contain myself, I poked myself in the eye with my ascara wand and did my lips like Bette Davis . . . He flushed e toilet and went back to sleep.

I couldn't stop thinking about it. All day, every time I looked him I saw him differently. I tried to talk to my husband about but he didn't understand because he had seen him naked on regular basis and he knew firsthand exactly what happens at irteen! Susie Vigas was terribly uninformed on this one. My usband thought I was making a big deal out of all this. The ardest part was knowing that I had a child who could father a hild and that in a certain way I had said good-bye to a whole ig piece of his life. It was a huge passage for me as a mother.)ften when the big changes in their lives come it isn't quite so obvious. My firstborn was now a young man and I wasn't quite eady for the physical changes that were coming. This must be unique to the parents of the opposite sex. It doesn't happen with fathers and sons and it doesn't happen with mothers and daughters. I'm simply confused. Bathing together is one day so natural, and the next day taboo. At six years old it's okay, but at seven it's not? When's the cutoff date? I know, I know, *most* children will feel the awkwardness on their own and want privacy for themselves and the change happens gradually. I'm just saying, what if they don't? What if they are perfectly content to see me naked until I'm ninety? I asked my oldest son what he thought. He said, "Mom, you are confusing seeing you naked with seeing someone cute naked. They're two totally different things." Should I have been relieved or offended?

What Did We Get?

*I*n fourth grade in California, they teach the history of our state. Much of that curriculum is based on the famous California missions. The culmination of that generally ends with that project that every parent in California has come to dread: the building of one of the missions. You see, I'm an art major . . . and this fired me up, not to mention there was a little of my own childhood baggage tied up in this project as well. I built San Juan Batista when I was in the fourth grade, but my mother would only let us build ours out of sugar cubes, so it ended up looking more like a Spanish-style igloo than an adobe mission. Mind you, mine was the ninth mission to pass through r doors, so now I understand her lack of enthusiasm. When y son hit fourth grade, I was excited for him. I took the chal-nge on a personal level. I would overcompensate for my lack the proper building materials by getting him all the good uff. I made sure to steer him toward choosing a mission that ad a little graveyard on the side. Those little crosses were so in to build.

We spent hours at the model store. I was choosing exactly ne right color of molding clay to match Father Junípero erra's motif. They had all kinds of neat little trees and even ed tile to use for the roof. Bryce stayed with it for about five ninutes, then I realized after about an hour had passed that he vas in the train section and I was still looking for miniature ani-nal hide material. We bought all the stuff and took it home ind began to build. Well, I began to build. Bryce went outside with his Rollerblades. I worked on the Mission San Rafael on and off for about a week. Bryce would come in every now and then to say, "It looks too good, make it look like I made it myself." I couldn't, it was all so perfect I couldn't not get an A. I painstakingly glued every tile to the roof, I even put little Indian women in the pews inside the church. I had purged my adolescent loss and recovered it through the Mission San Rafael.

Bryce took it to school and came home that same day with the mission in his arms. I said eagerly, "What'd we get?" He said, "I got an A, Mom, but guess what? We didn't have to build a whole mission, we just had to bring in something from the Mission period. Some kids just had baskets, some kids just drew a picture. We did all that work for nothing!"

"*We* didn't do anything . . . I made that mission, you Rollerbladed, remember? And it wasn't for nothing . . . We got a lot out of it."

He threw the work of art in the backseat and slammed the door, crushing the entire graveyard.

This was simply the beginning of the projects that we would share, with me always getting way more involved than I should. It's just that when you are doing a science project on rodents, there are typefaces that seem to say "rodent" more than others. Keeping my little paws out of it is getting harder and harder to do. I know why I get so involved. Some would say it's because I want my child's self-esteem to improve, that I want him to feel successful. Well, actually, for me it is none of those things. It's all about me, it's because I get to have all the knowledge and wisdom of an adult as a child, sort of. Okay, okay, I understand that I have to let them do it alone.

This year Eric did his science project totally by himself from beginning to end. Honestly. The day he was gluing down the headings onto the presentation board crooked, I had to bite my tongue and hold my hands behind my back, but I did it. I have to admit that he got a much greater sense of satisfaction out of doing it himself. Here's the catch. When the judges were done giving out the awards at the science fair, Eric only got a second-place ribbon among a sea of obviously parentally co-oped first-place entries, projects with concepts that would rival NASA technology. He was devastated. The only thing that both of us took home was the belief that these so-called extra projects have become a joke. I had been right getting involved, because unfortunately the blue ribbon was a measure not of what the child knows, understands and did alone, but of whose parents knew where to buy the best stuff and knew the differences and subtleties of typefaces. Unfortunately for Eric, Bodoni Ultra Bold doesn't say "earthquake." He'll learn. Mommy is here.

agree with Caryl: an adult mind is a terrible thing to waste.

I was with her when her oldest got the blue ribbon on the science project. She came running out of her dressing room yelling, "We got first place!"

The whole cast and crew of *The Mommies* turned and asked, "WE?"

I was also with her when Eric got second place for his "untouched" science project. She was so mad at the parents who "cheated."

Any mother who says she doesn't live through her children is lying to herself. We may not recognize it in ourselves, but come on, we all know who *really* has an investment in getting the A on the science report. I helped Aaron make an elaborate snake report once when he was in seventh grade and he frustrated me so badly because he never bothered to find out what grade I got on it.

When he was in third grade, Aaron wanted to be a gladiator for Halloween. I cleverly and painstakingly made every bit of that elaborate costume: papier-mâché helmet, cardboard vest, little metal skirt, shield, sword and all. I was so proud of my artwork. For a brief moment I fancied the idea of sending Charlton Heston a photograph of Aaron in all his glory.

The Chamber of Commerce held a judged costume parade in downtown Petaluma that year and, of course, I entered Charlton—I mean, Aaron. It was an average year as far as costumes were concerned. All the usual pumpkins, pirates and princesses marched to the tune of "The Teddy Bears' Picnic" in front of the judges. We had it all over them. My gladiator glowed with creativity, elaborate costuming details, originality. I was beaming. All Aaron wanted to know was when the good candy was coming out. "Later, honey, later. Now go march nicely in front of the judges." When it came time for the first place winner, I held my breath. "And first place goes to . . ."

My heart was pounding.

". . . the vampire!"

The vampire? The VAMPIRE? Whose kid was the damn vampire? A beaming mom hugged her child. How unoriginal. I figured she must have slept with the mayor or something. I was crushed. I just stood there and cried. Aaron asked if he could go get his candy. Unable to speak, I pitifully nodded.

My mother always wanted to take dance lessons. During the Depression years when she was a child, it was beyond impossible to indulge in that dream. She waited six long years after I was born, then enrolled me in ballet, tap and jazz. She never dropped me off, but went in and watched every lesson. My little dance recitals were a big deal in my house. I really loved it, though, and felt her love, as well. So what if she was living through my little legs?

When my boys were in elementary school, I longed for old-fashioned school plays about Miles Standish wooing Priscilla, but the teachers were already overloaded and didn't share my sentimentality. I wanted to sit in that audience, hanky to eye, and feel the joy my mother did when my little ballet slippers touched the stage during the Christmas recital at the old folks' home. So I took it upon myself to write, direct and choreograph grand epic musicals like *Gone With the Petaluma Wind*. Caryl began calling me Signora Fellini. Every single child in the school had a part in

plays, mind you. Every mother had her thrill. My boys, of
[cou]rse, were prominently displayed.

I knew nothing about directing a play, which
[I l]ater learned was much like it is here in
[Ho]llywood. No, I did *not* walk around town
[wi]th a cape and beret, as Caryl might like you
[to] think, but I did have a lot of glue guns
[an]d yellow chicken feathers in my purse (I
[al]ways incorporated chickens in my
[th]eme).

After the very successful *Gone With
[th]e Petaluma Wind*, I was gearing up for
[B]*en-Her* when I hit a little snag. The
[pr]oblem was with my boys. They
[di]dn't want to star in anyone's play,
[le]t alone their mother's. They also
[k]new I was living their life on the
[st]age and told me to get an out-
[le]t. I did and that's how *The
[M]ommies* came about.

Once a mother's fulfilled
[i]n those matters, it's hard to
"get it up" for the remain-
[i]ng children. When we
[f]irst moved to L.A., seven-
[y]ear-old Marcy thought
[s]he wanted to take acting
[l]essons. Every Saturday
morning, after a couple
of hours of drama exer-

I was so proud; he just wanted candy.

cises with the masochistic teacher made parents sit
through the whole taping of the class.

There was our little Miss Marcy standing with four other taller, talented, budding thespians. Their assignment was become a seed planted in rich soil. I saw four children crouch down in a compact ball on the floor and one daughter stand with her hands on her hips looking distastefully down at others. As the seeds began to sprout, Marcy shifted her weight from one foot to the other. She looked at the growing flower on either side of her, then stared right into the camera with such a look of criticism I thought I was looking into a mirror.

We could hear the teacher's voice: "Wind. There's a gentle breeze . . ." and the flowers began to sway. Marcy moved the hair that was in front of her ear and tucked it neatly behind. was about all she could muster up for a fantasy breeze.

This was pure agony for me. I just wanted to yell at the video piece, "Sprout, damn it!"

We only went to about five of those torture sessions, then gratefully, Marcy saw that it was not her calling. Some kids never do. My heart goes out to those mothers.

We all live through our children in some way, shape or form. Sure, we jump at the chance to condemn the Patsy Ramseys of the world, but I think if we're all honest about it, it's a very short trip between beauty pageant moms and soccer parents' dragging our preadolescents across the ountry to compete. Veiled in the shroud of "Athletic activity is ood for kids" and "Life is about competition" could be the fact nat most of us as children never came close to doing anything iearly as exciting. At ten years old, most of us were staging our wn beauty pageants in our garages and charging the neigh- orhood kids to watch. So one mother puts makeup and cos- umes on her daughter and makes her perform like a profes- ional adult model and the other puts cleats and shin guards on ier daughter and expects her to have the composure and drive of a professional athlete. We judge them against adult stan- dards in both arenas. It's all a matter of how far do you take it and how much and when do you pull back.

Every now and then, either my husband or I must point out to the other that maybe we have become a little too invested for our own good. That maybe when I silently mouthed Eric's sixth-grade class election speech, word for word, as he was doing it meant that I should pull back a tad. Some of the best parental moments have come standing on the sidelines and watching your little one rise above the challenge and come out a winner. I've been there with tears in my eyes watching my sons accept awards for things that made their father and me happier than they were. They usually toss the trophy in the trunk and never look back, but I've caught my husband giving tours of our house and lingering a little too long in the trophy section. Last time I had to whisper to him gently, "Honey, those aren't your trophies."

I've also seen them perform like seasoned stand-up comedi- ans working a room to great applause, and my own heart melts, because somehow I get the credit. Whether it is real or imagined, I simply know that it is a direct reflection on my par- enting skills. Their rewards are our rewards. It's only when you

catch yourself actually wearing their crowns and posing in th
mirror that they should haul you away to an institution fo
"Adults Looking for Accolades." I hope that Marilyn and I ca
at least room together when we get there.

---

*The Mommies' Five Warning Signs That You
Might Be Living Through Your Kids*

1. You show up for class pictures.

2. You sleep with their trophies.

3. You sleep with their coach. (Unless their coach
   is their father, then you hold back on sex until
   they make your child the star.)

4. You find yourself trying to squeeze into their
   little costumes whenever they're not around.

5. You hire a hit man to rub out the competition.

The Seven Virtues

What do I value most? I believe that there's nothing better than a great pair of shoes, thick, silky hair and any sandwich made with Best Foods mayonnaise. I've been shallow for pretty much all my life. Even in the sixties, living in a commune, I remained true to my shallow self. Sure, we were often embroiled in discussions about how the government was profiting from the Vietnam War, why we believed our parents' generation were a bunch of alcoholic hypocrites, how incredible it seemed that someone could take another human's life and the awful truth about how the whites screwed the Indian Nation. If you looked closely, I was passionately carrying on my side the debate while bleaching the hair on my legs.

When Marcy was around eight years old, I was combi͏ṇg her hair in front of the bathroom mirror and, in my never-en͏d͏ing quest to provide her with higher self-esteem, I asked wh͏a͏t she liked most about her face.

She hesitated and said shyly, "Well, I guess I like m͏y mouth," then, "What do you like best about your face͏, Mommy?"

I looked into the mirror and said readily, "My eye job." S͏o much for modeling self-acceptance.

Every school year at Back to School Night, while th͏e teacher is explaining her philosophy and curriculum, I'm judg͏ing her on her choice of shoes. White pumps usually mean it'͏s going to be a difficult year.

The Law of Nature says: Shallow mothers beget shal-low daughters. Too bad Marcy was developing her value system while I was doing the talk show, because whenever she had her little friends over, she felt compelled to give them a complete makeover. She even gave away her own clothes. I suppose she didn't want to be like our cheap show and make her guests give back everything after it was all over. She was a "real friend."

I was trying to remember the Seven Virtues from the Bible. I guess I need a refresher course because I could only come up with Modesty, Honesty, Patience, Intelligence, Humility and what's the one where you're not supposed to sleep with anyone else but your husband? Chastity. I was lost, so I called a religious expert: Caryl's mom, Claire. She told me that there wasn't a list of exactly seven virtues and that I was probably thinking of the seven deadly sins. Recalling Brad Pitt and Morgan Freeman, I think maybe she was right. She also told me that

telligence was a gift, not a virtue. She very nicely reminded me that unfortunately intelligence is inherited, that some people were born with limits. I was waiting for her to say, "Present company excluded," but she never did.

Shallow flower children.

My mother's values are so down-to-earth. There's an accustomed quality of modesty. I'm talking about living modestly and remaining perfectly content. I was grocery shopping the other day when I was hit in my heart by a clear picture of how things have changed. I was in a hurry; my daughter was running a fever and I was throwing fruit and 7UP quickly into my

cart. Then I noticed an older white-haired woman, frail as yo
could imagine, looking lovingly at some muffins. She had on
bag of frozen cauliflower in her left hand and some cannin
wax in the right. Apparently the muffins weren't in he
coupon envelope. Maybe she was just weighing her options
Although it would probably only serve as some sort of insult
I just wanted to buy the muffins for her and skate right on by
any poignant, sad feelings. I just wanted to fix it.

I think there's a lot to learn from an era that taught these
beautiful women that food might be sparse and canning is one
way to deal with it. I have no idea whatsoever how to can
something and the only things that are in my freezer right now
are a few Lean Cuisines, some ice cream sandwiches and a bottle of vodka. I suppose one could call that living modestly. But
who am I trying to kid? I'm from a world that says, "If my four-
year-old poops in his corduroy pants, throw away the
pants. Avoid the pants. Do not touch the pants." I'm a
wimp. Do you know how many wet, dirty diapers stewing
in a toilet our mothers had to touch so our little soft, round
butts didn't get a rash? Those cloth diapers lived on in our houses for many years after, too. Oh, yes, I recycle, but it's really
bourgeois recycling where I simply separate stuff, barely touching it, into three bins and bring it to the sidewalk. Okay, I have
my husband bring it to the sidewalk. I have never darned a sock.

Is frugality one of the virtues? I hate sales. I figure if
nobody else wanted those damn dresses, then I certainly don't.
My mother can stretch a dollar all the way to Heaven. She is the
queen of the garage sales. Is your mother like that, too? My
mother hangs all the rubber bands from the daily paper on a
doorknob and then when the paper boy comes collecting, she
gives them back to him neatly in a Baggie. He just stares at her.
He doesn't know what to do.

Okay, maybe I don't live by those virtues and I admit I do judge women who still perm their hair, but not all is shallow in my world. I know what qualities I value in other people.

These are my Seven Virtues:

#1. I admire people whose actions show that they put *Family First:* The single mom who drags herself out of bed the one morning she gets to sleep in to make sure those kids go with her to church. The dad who comes home early on a Friday night with a bucket of Kentucky Fried Chicken in one hand and some Uno cards in the other.

#2. I think it's a virtue to be *Neighborly.* It's important that we take care of each other, don't you think? Modern conveniences make it so easy to stay isolated, and it seems that all too often we miss out on connecting with some good folks. Everybody has an interesting story if we just ask.

#3. I admire my friends who don't know what's on TV. I think to be *Well Read* is a virtue. I'm not talking about that group of insecure people who have to put on the highbrow intellectual bravado. Isn't it irritating when the well-read show-off implies with a simple tone of voice that you're not quite in her league? That takes her right out of the virtue category. I appreciate the kind of entertaining readers that pepper their conversations with interesting bits of information that will get us thinking, and I don't mean just reports from *People,* either. I get that on my own.

#4. I respect any one who has *Willpower.* I want to know their secret. They can, and do, pass right on by the blinking yellow arrow that points to Burgers! Burgers! Burgers! I just

don't know how they do it. How do they keep their hands ou
of the trick-or-treat bag late at night?

#5. *The Ability to Laugh at Yourself* is a wonderfu
virtue. It doesn't come into our lives until after the teen year:
Teenagers tend to lose their sense of humor altogether. T
appreciate the humor in our own foibles is so endearing.

#6. People who have *Passion* are to be admired. I have
cousin who loves birds. She volunteers at the bird rescue,
cleans the oil off pelicans. Birds of prey are her favorites. Every
year at our family reunion she tests our bird knowledge. She
would rather go see a bald eagle's nest than go shopping. I love
that about her.

#7. And the seventh virtue is to be *Photogenic*. I admire
anyone who can look good in any photograph, whether it's
early in the morning or straight out in sunlight. The world is a
brighter place because of these people.

You can always count on me to get back to my shallow
roots.

This Is a Test . . .
It Is Only a Test!

There are days when it seems as though I am the only one doing anything to keep this household running. The grunt work, if you will. Being that I am the only one in my house who is genetically predisposed to picking up a broom, I begin to make sweeping generalizations (no pun intended) about the opposite sex and their ineptness in the home hygiene department. I always wonder what the place would end up looking like if I died. Would they actually never take the dead and molding flowers out of the vase? Would they really never change the sheets on the beds? Would they just wash the dishes on a need-to-use basis only? Could they honestly, in my memory, use that same worn-out greasy sponge to wash the kitchen counters over and over and over again? Only to hit the floor with it periodically, too? I marvel at their ability to go days, weeks and sometimes even months without putting something away, something that they must purposely step over, around, or avoid altogether in order to go along their merry way.

In fact, it is so curious to me that sometimes I will run my own test on the subject. Last summer, for instance, someone had been out sunning himself using a number 4 SPF tanning oil. When finished, as always, he left it in the middle of the deck, in the pathway to the door. That person shall remain nameless. Let's just say he is past his physical prime and his tan isn't the basis of my love for him. Well, that bottle sat in that same place for weeks. I was determined not to pick it up. I wanted to see exactly how long it would take for someone other than myself to put it away. Now mind you, several of my women friends and my sister had come to visit and even they always made attempts to pick the bottle up on their way across the deck. One by one I had to stop them and let them in on my little test. They would laugh and share similar stories of the same things at their homes. I was comforted by their camaraderie and even more so when they would call, sometimes weeks later, to see the status of the test. "Hi, Caryl, how's the test going?" "It's still there . . . I guess he wants to know where it will be next summer."

This went on from late July to early October, and then I snapped. I just couldn't take it anymore. I had to put it back where it belonged. Still, the oily little ring that it left is a constant reminder to me that no one else cares about these little things. When I see the oily ring, I think *Lord of the Flies*.

When I came clean and told my husband about the test, he said, "I landscaped the whole backyard and all you can think bout is that I didn't put the suntan lotion away. That is ridiculous! Why didn't you just ask me to put it away?"

I guess he has a point, but my rebuttal to that is "If you can wheelbarrow four yards of topsoil into the backyard, why can't you simply bend over and pick up the damned suntan lotion?" I think that is the more logical point, don't you? I tried to explain that it's all the little things that we do that make our houses homes. Keeping the house clean lets us live with dignity, and if someone never put something away after they used it, we would end up living like one of those ladies who have a thousand cats with feces scattered all over the place.

That's why it matters that the table looks nice when it's set for dinner. It's why there are candles in the bathroom and potted plants and picture frames around. If life was full of just what we needed to survive, we would be the Swiss Family Robinson. It's the same reason that you encourage me to get out of my sweatpants every now and then. (I think I finally got to him on that last one.) He acted as if he got the connection, anyway.

Never one to let it go, I decided to see how long it would take him to throw away the empty shampoo bottles in the shower. I'll keep you posted.

I believe that in order to communicate your ideas clearly, more words are better than fewer words and one word is better than a grunt. This past Halloween I was working on this very book and it was Len's day to pick Eric up at school. He wandered into my office at about 2:15 and said, "I wish I could get somebody to pick Eric up." Well, because I was deep into the book, I didn't pick up on what that simple little statement really meant. Normally my antenna would have been fully extended and I would have known that he had another agenda, like the football game at my other son's high school, but I didn't. Instead I took it at its face value. I thought he had been driving around all day and wouldn't it be great if he didn't have to drive the ten miles again that day. Taking pity on him, I said, "If you really want, I'll stop writing and go and get him." He merely grunted and walked out of the room. I thought I saw him shrug, feeling guilty for interrupting my work. My interpretation was that he was still getting Eric. It was one of those unfinished conversations we always seem to have.

Then at about twenty minutes to three I saw his truck back out of the driveway. I guess he went to get him. I went back to the book. I hadn't looked at the clock until the phone rang. It was five o'clock on Halloween night and Eric was calling from school saying, "Mommy . . . I'm the last one here. Why hasn't Daddy come to get me?"

My heart sank. "Eric, he left two hours ago. I don't know where he could possibly be." I tried paging him three times until I heard the pager rattling from its vibration on the kitchen counter. Why wouldn't he have taken his pager? I started to worry that he had been in an accident. I couldn't leave to get Eric because I was waiting for the call from my other son, who needed a ride home after the football game. I imposed on a friend who was busy getting her kids into costume to pick up Eric. It's always the girlfriend who bails you out and gives you that "You are well within your rights to kill him" kind of encouragement. Suddenly I put it all together. I knew he had gone to that game . . . and he grunted about me picking Eric up because he didn't want to really face the fact that maybe my work was more important than his attendance at a football game where he knew no one playing!

My friend called to say she had Eric and asked, "Have you heard from Len? Do you think he's okay?" to which I replied, "Unfortunately . . . either way he's a dead man!"

I drove to the high school looking for the "foggy language" man, where I found a jubilant Len rooting on the last play of the game.

He said, "Hey, what are you doing here?" all happy, as if I were there as a booster. "You were supposed to get Eric, remember?" I screamed.

He said, "You told me that you would pick him up."

"I offered to pick him up in a conversation that we never finished! And why did you leave out the part about coming to the football game? You see, in order for me to understand that you wanted me to pick him up, that would require more words than a grunt and go. It's Halloween and your son is all alone at school while the rest of the world is trick-or-treating and besides, every woman who rescued us tonight said it was your fault." He went silent. He knows better than to fight the Women's Union.

Nothing Works

An Act of Discipline

*T*he notion of disciplining someone else, even if it's my own kid, is so irritating. It's not as if I don't enjoy bossing people around. I'm a firstborn child, it's my nature to take charge. It's just that no one listens to me, especially my kids. Obedience is not in any fiber of my children's being. They wouldn't have lasted two weeks had they been born in China.

When I was twenty-six and pregnant with Aaron, my discipline techniques included visualization, guided meditation and yoga. I pictured myself sitting with this precious little soul and teaching him the study of spiritual awakening, the subtle differences between meditation and self-hypnosis and perhaps the fine art of astral travel. I anticipated that all I really needed was the bond between mother and child; that love alone would serve as my fundamental guide while I walked him through the formative years of life. Then I had him.

First of all, Aaron didn't seem to be able to hold still. I couldn't even get him to breathe deeply. He would *not* get esoteric with me. All he wanted was trucks, shovels and guns. He worshipped dirt. At first I saw his love for the soil as his way of getting in touch with Mother Earth. However, it soon became apparent that he just wanted to make little Mother Earth balls and throw them at neighbor kids. He was not how I imagined my child would be. Okay, I did tap-dance the whole time I was pregnant, which gave him a great sense of rhythm. Could I have accidentally shaken him up too much?

I don't know where I got the idea that all I had to do was ask him *nicely* not to destroy the other yards in our cul-de-sac and explain *logically* why we don't crush neighbors' flowers with our Big Wheels and he would respond sensibly, but nothing I tried worked. I had a long road ahead of me, and it was not exactly the path to Nirvana.

When Aaron was two our family went out to dinner at a Chinese restaurant to celebrate his grandmother's birthday. As usual, he went around to every family member and took a little to eat from each plate. I guess I would call that style of discipline my "Helen Keller Approach." Once in a while he strayed from our table and tried to get some egg rolls from other diners. I would run over apologetically and guide him back our way, always sporting that "isn't he just too cute?" look of a first-time mother. This story is downright embarrassing, but I must go on. I got up to leave with Baby Aaron in my arms, instructing him to wave bye-bye to Grandma. Everyone in the restaurant, including the staff, applauded his departure.

This "Blind Mother syndrome" of mine went on for some years. When Aaron was in second grade, I kissed him good-bye one chilly March morning. As he got on the bus for Old Adobe Elementary School, I began to wonder if he was trying to tell me something. He entered the classroom sporting the uniform he had worn every day for the previous four months. It was his own special uniform: full World War II combat gear, camouflage shirt, pants, hard helmet and all. He looked like he belonged on Rat Patrol as he put away his backpack, grenades and canteen. That morning I thought perhaps he might be unconsciously asking to be sent to military school. I realized then that perhaps a little more structure in our lives would be helpful.

I began attending weekly classes at the Family Education Center, where I was to spend the next ten years being educated in the Rudolf Dreikurs/Alfred Adler style of positive discipline. About twelve desperate moms and an occasional dad met every Wednesday afternoon to get advice on how to handle our little tyrants.

The best part about taking parenting classes is that you get to find out that your kid is not the most obnoxious one. I loved that part. Sometimes I didn't even pay attention to the techniques I was supposed to learn. I just liked to hear how some other kid fought with his brother nonstop, or said "Look at me. Look at me. Look at me" nonstop or still pooped in his pants . . . nonstop.

I became a parenting class maniac. My favorite disciplinary tool was the logical and natural consequence. A natural consequence is when a parent gets out of the way between the child's action and what occurs as the natural effect. For example, if a fourth grader forgets his lunch, the natural result is that he goes hungry for a couple of hours. Mom "gets out of the way" by not running a sandwich over to the school. Usually, from then on, he remembers to bring his lunch. A logical consequence is when a parent steps in and does the logical action as it relates to the problem. Here's an example that would come in handy if, say, you've got a dawdling preschooler: First you explain to him the night before that the car leaves, with him in it, at exactly eight o'clock in the morning whether or not he's ready. Next comes the hard part: You follow through. No nagging, no reminding. If he's still in his jammies, he goes to preschool in jammies. A logical consequence is not the same as a punishment, and the child need not necessarily suffer to learn. It is my contention that it is the parent who suffers. I hate following through. Following through is for the strong. I only like to follow through when it's easy.

M

The teachers at the Family Education Center were taken aback by the way I tried out my logical consequence: One evening, I asked Aaron, then eight, and Richie, nine, to come in from play and set the table, their regular family chore. They responded with the familiar singsong, "In a minute." "In a minute" in young-boy time means indefinitely. I tried once more. Getting the same response, I simply placed the dinner—pork chops, mashed potatoes with gravy, peas, applesauce, biscuits and all—directly on the kitchen table. No forks, no knives, no spoons, no plates, not even a napkin.

"Dinner's ready!" I called out in the same singsong voice from my place at the table. My husband and kids came to the table and stopped short.

"I don't think you'll be wanting milk tonight," I suggested with a little smile.

The boys in unison responded, "Cool!"

My husband gave me a tentative, confused look; then they all joined me. The boys dug in. The adults ate gingerly. We scooped up mashed potatoes with our pork chop bones, lifted each salad leaf with our fingers. The boys went straight down on the table like it was a trough. How natural. They licked, scooped and sucked it all right off the Formica. And as much as they enjoyed their meal in the wild, they didn't love clearing the table. Honestly, I never again had to ask them twice to set it. I loved this parenting technique!

It didn't stop there, either. I found that natural and logical consequences worked quite well on my husband, my neighbors, my colleagues at work, my husband's ex-wife, the clerk behind the cash register—hell, I even had some success on the cat.

The positive discipline techniques sustained me for many years, but teenagers who think they're omnipotent aren't concerned with consequences set by their mothers. They scoff at them. They roll their eyes at them. And in my case, they laugh at them.

One late morning after all the kids had gone to school, I was in the drive-through line at McDonald's when I saw seventeen-year-old Aaron cross right in front of my car toward the entrance of the building. Shocked, I honked. He realized it was me and, unlike most teens who get caught cutting school, he smiled and waved excitedly.

"Hi, Mom! What are *you* doing here? Can you give me a ride to Joey's?" he happily blurted out.

"What do you mean, what am I doing here? What are *you* doing here? Why aren't you in school? No, I will not give you a ride to Joey's. Get in the car. I'm taking you right back to school! And why aren't you afraid of me? Damn it!"

Nothing Works   163

I have actually said no to my kids in their lifetime. Okay,
can name the times on two hands. Kids know all too well ho⌐
to be relentless and we sucker in just to shut them up. I am th⌐
worst. I want my kids to be happy, happy, happy. I know
should be strong and build their character, but I have n⌐
patience for it. I depend on their father to be the strong one
but all too often he has no clue as to what they're talking about

I came home late one night. Richard was home with the
teens and baby Marcy. First I went into the family room, where
the TV was blasting. There were four sixteen-year-old boys sitting on my couch, all strangers to me. I asked them where
Aaron was and they pointed upstairs. I peeked in his room and
as I opened the door, his friend Joey jumped to a sitting position on the floor. The girl he had been lying on scurried to a sitting position as well. I looked over to see my son lying on his
water bed looking like a voyeur. I said, "What's going on
here?" I then heard a little voice coming from under
Aaron. "Hi, Mrs. Kentz."

"Is that you, Darlene?"

She wiggled out from under him. "I guess I better go now."

"Yes, I guess you had better. As a matter of fact, could you
all leave? Aaron, where's your father?"

"Oh, he's asleep."

Sometimes it's my liberalism that gets in the way of disciplining my kids. I was folding Aaron's laundry one day when he
was a junior in high school and I came across a pair of girl's
panties. My conservative friends would have taken him to task
about his sex life and somehow grounded him, then sent him
to another country for some missionary work. My first
thought, on the other hand, was, "Oh no, I hope he's not been
wearing these."

Times have changed so much. I don't believe in spanking a

hild. Spanking is hitting. My father used to hit me with a belt. My mother would eye the belt she had hanging in the kitchen and we would quickly obey. It was the norm, not thought of as abuse then at all. I don't even carry sour memories of the punishments. It's just that I couldn't do that to my child. I also don't think spanking works. Now, squeezing their little arm is another story. No, I'm kidding. I have been known to squeeze out of frustration. It's usually when we're in a store and my kids are grabbing things off the shelves, jamming themselves under the cart and whining for Froot Loops. My daughter would bust me every time. "You're squeezing my arm! YOU'RE SQUEEZING MY ARM!"

I love those moms who discipline in another language. While I'm smiling and gritting my teeth as two-year-old Marcy throws herself on the ground because she doesn't want to leave the birthday party, Mrs. Abergel is rattling off commands in French that probably say, "See that kid crying over there? That's what you'll look like if we don't leave immediately!" and no one knows the difference.

Disciplining your children is a personal thing. There are no hard-and-fast rules that bring on some magical Stepford child. If mutual respect is your goal, you'll find it. Just remember to follow through. Well, SOMEBODY'S got to follow through.

My Little Monarch

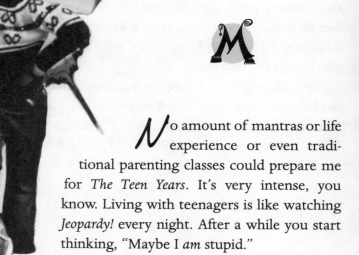

No amount of mantras or life experience or even traditional parenting classes could prepare me for *The Teen Years*. It's very intense, you know. Living with teenagers is like watching *Jeopardy!* every night. After a while you start thinking, "Maybe I *am* stupid."

Beware. One afternoon you might be in your favorite chair taking your first break of the day, reading a magazine, feeling relaxed and content. Then your teen will enter the room and say something like "Hey, I'm oing out tonight." You'll look up quizzically with no agenda whatsoever and he'll accuse you of attacking him. In a tone meant only for an idiot, he'll spew, "Jeez, you don't have to stress about it!" An adolescent can bring you to the emotion of rage faster than anyone you'll ever meet in your whole life. If your babies are still small, just wait. It's strange when you find yourself thinking, "This is my baby. I have loved him, I have nurtured him, I have protected him and now I hate him." Oh, well.

When Aaron was a teen, I would experience moments of fear, usually around three in the morning, that *he* was the embodiment of all that was wrong with society today.

Clearly Aaron's emphasis in high school was the short-term female relationship. It's what got him up in the morning. Ah, if only there existed a grading system for that. He was sort of the Bill Clinton of Casa Grande High. And like Bill, he's had a couple of real sweethearts pop up lately to say hi. Some of his girlfriends stand out in my memory more than others. Actually, I liked them all, once I got to know them. Some stayed only long enough for a date and a color-coordinated wrist corsage and boutonniere, others became part of our family. The breakup usually was harder on me than anyone else.

I recall it was Amber who was his first high school love. Amber called him so often, we rented the old Clint Eastwood movie *Play Misty for Me* to warn him where the relationship might be headed. Amber is the reason we had to cancel call-waiting.

There was Miss Petaluma, better known in our house as "Little Miss Hickey." Too bad we never had a snakebite emergency. Man, she was a Hoover vacuum just sucking away on his neck. One day I answered the phone when she called and I said, "Boy, can you suck!" A very horrified Aaron grabbed the receiver.

I caught him dabbing the suck marks with my makeup, but I don't think even Wite-Out could cover those puppies. Their relationship didn't last too long, though. I asked him if it was because her vacuum bag got too full and she lost her sucking power, but Aaron said it was mainly because of her many Miss Petaluma duties and a prior commitment to the Dairy Festival.

Next was Tiffany, wonder cheerleader, who was always lying on him. Maybe she was just tired from cheering so much, I don't know, but every time I walked into the family room, she was lying on my son. No one popped up. No one blushed. They just kept on having their little chat. They seemed so compatible. And happy. They were both fully clothed, mind you, she in school-spirit colors, he in ripped jeans.

Unbelievable as it might seem, it did shock this flower-wearing, summer-of-naked-loving hippie-turned-mother. I felt very uncomfortable standing there holding a bag of groceries while they told me about their day, the activities that were coming up, who won the game. I'd end up saying, "So, Tiffany, looks like you're staying for dinner again. Why don't you get *off* him and help me set the table?"

He got a little more serious in his senior year. Her name was Stacy. One day in June just before graduation, he came home and announced that he and Stacy were going to get married. I really loved Stacy. She was smart and cute and friendly. She was taking all honors classes and intended to go on to college to become a pharmacist . . . and Aaron did have asthma. I thought, "Well, he would always have inhalers." But is that enough of a reason to get married? I don't know. Remember, I got married to my first husband when I was his age and my reason was much more risky than a possible future with Ventolin. There was no need for Aaron and Stacy to go through a struggling marriage when they could do like any other couple in the ineties: live together. So when Aaron made his big marriage announcement, I said, "Why don't you tell Stacy to come live with us? I mean, she's been lying on you all year anyway. What's the difference, really?"

Three days later, Stacy moved in. She had a lot of clothes and boxes. I could hear Aaron overhead upstairs pacing back and forth while she was rearranging his—excuse me, *their*—room. After a while, he came to me with a miffed look and started that controlled shout/whisper thing: "Now, I didn't mind it when she brought in a flowery bedcover, I didn't mind it when she hooked up that dumb Mickey Mouse phone, and I *sort of* didn't mind it when she took down my beer can pyramid. But, Mom, there . . . are . . . *bunnies* on my bed!" I'm not sure, but I thought I saw a tear.

Trying hard to hold back a grin, I slowly turned around and gently reminded, "It's not your bed anymore. Why, son, I think you've just learned the first rule of marriage . . . *You don't get to decorate!* Soon she'll be sponging your walls. You know that faux finish on every 'hip' wall on our cul-de-sac?"

He nodded forlornly.

"That was done by a woman with a sponge. You see, we rulers of the suburbs are extremely cunning. We can take an ordinary sponge, wipe down a sink, add a little acrylic paint, dab it on the wall and then at night use it for contraception. You won't know what hit you!"

The relationship ran its full course and everyone was thankful not to have to hire divorce lawyers or seek mediation. As usual, I was more upset than anyone else. The breakup went fairly smoothly. Stacy simply took her bunnies and left. New beer cans went up and the parties began.

Parties hosted by teenagers are every parent's nightmare. It's a rare household that's never had a covert kegger come across their door. These days the kids charge their guests, no only for the drinks, but also for the housekeeper they hire t clean up after their young butts. My son was notorious for hav ing good parties. My husband and I finally had to stop all ou weekend activities. Even if we hired an adult to guard the house while we attended a Marriage Encounter, Aaron would figure out a way to sneak a party.

I went to a friend's one evening and when I introduced myself to the baby-sitter, she said, "Oh, I know who you are. I've seen your picture." So I questioned her as to where she could have seen my photograph and she said, "Oh, at Aaron's party last Friday." Then I went into Kinko's and the young gentleman at the counter taking my money said, "Hey, aren't you Aaron's mom? Cool party." I became paranoid. Was I the *only* one not invited to his little fund-raiser? (How do you think he got his spending money?) Then there was the day I was sure the girl taking my order at McDonald's was smirking. Had she been making out on my bed or something? The sweater she was wearing looked familiar. Could it have been mine? Richard and I never went out again after that. We became mighty grateful for pizza and Blockbuster Video.

A teenager's mood is ten times his body weight. Even fifteen-year-olds have a hugeness about them. Everyone—family members, your friends, pets, etc.—all know when a teen has entered a room. You might be playing Yahtzee or laughing over old home videos and the room will suddenly become still. You look around at each other and then back to the adolescent as if to say, "What's it going to be today? A happy happy teen day? Or will you try to tear us down, one by one?"

As much as you deny it, your teen has the power. Most of the time they're simply trying to survive, swimming out of control, getting tossed around by the hormonal ebb and flow, nd we just happen to get in the way. Other times their new-ound power amuses them and they try to toy with you.

I remember one day when I was having two of my col-eagues from work over for a little luncheon. It was important o me that we be left alone for three whole hours. I had asked Aaron to please not interrupt me at all during this time. Just as I was serving the quiche, in walks Mr. Power. He pulls out a couple of frozen corn dogs, slips them into the microwave and pours himself a tall glass of Gatorade. Through clenched teeth, I asked, "What do you think you're doing?"

"Oh, nothing, really. I just thought I'd hang with you guys for a little while."

"I told you I wanted to be left alone for three hours."

"Hey, what's the big deal? Can't a guy get a bite to eat in this house? Jeez, I'm hungry, that's all." Then he grabbed his meal and sat down.

My friends were staring at their plates. I sat down near them and said, "Boy, I just got my period this morning and *am I flow-ing*! Don't you just hate it when you don't know whether to use a nighttime pad or a regular or one with wings?"

Bev chimed in, "I don't know if I should get scented or unscented . . . "

Aaron sat motionless, corn dog in his mouth, midbite, wincing. She went on, "Minipads or maxipads?"

I tried to add "Do you ever . . . " but before I finished my question, he had dropped his dog, cupped his hands over his ears and run right out of the house.

I don't always have my wits about me, though. Take curfew, for instance. Aaron's weekend curfew was midnight. I could never stay up that late, so I'd go to bed, sleeping lightly until he popped his head in our room and let me know he was safely home. When curfew time came at a party and he wanted to *stay* at the party, he would simply call home. I'd answer sleepily "Hello?" Then he'd say, "It's okay, Mom. I got it." Then I'd murmur, "Oh, okay," hang up and fall back to sleep, this time soundly, thinking he was home safe.

This little ploy worked for him until the night I had to stay up late to do some paperwork and he called with his usual "It's okay, Mom. I got it," and I said, "Yeah, you got it. You got restriction. Get home now."

Teenagers turn on you because they need to separate from you. It's their job, and face it, they do make it a little easier to plan for a future without them. But I tell you, one of the hardest things a mother has to do in her life is say good-bye to her baby. I know, I've done it twice. It's all about the vacant room. The quiet house. The empty lap.

M Sometimes I'll look into his grown-up eyes and I'll see that precious eight-year-old who was there with me just a minute ago. I can still see him standing on my front porch with a red sweatshirt, little camouflage shorts and wad of flowers in his hand that he had just picked from the neighbor's yard. Flowers meant for his mommy, with his arm outstretched and his eyes saying, "I adore you." I miss him. I still want to hold him. Watch out, those days go by so fast.

Even now, when I least expect it, I'll hear some young boy's voice calling out, "Mom!" and for a split second I think it's him, needing me. One night I was in our local Ralph's grocery store and I saw a sixteen-year-old boy and his mother doing the mom/kid dance: "Why can't I have it?"

"Because I said no."

"But, why?"

"Listen up, I said no."

"Can I get it with my own money?"

"No."

"Hey, you can't say no. It's my own money!"

They went on and I got sentimental. I went right home and called Aaron. Through tears, I made him promise to come visit the next weekend and go to Ralph's with me. I thought I could hear him rolling his eyes over the phone.

The weekend he came for a visit, we were preparing for friends of the family to come for dinner. We were all busy setting the table, fixing the food, ironing the tablecloth and so on when Aaron went over to the stereo, put on Patsy Cline and asked me for a slow dance. As he gracefully guided me, I noticed how tall he'd gotten. And handsome. Wearing my earrings. I can't hold him now, he holds me.

This slow dance was the beginning of the new relationship. The relationship we all hope for. One of laughter, friendship, shared and mutual respect. He's twenty-three now and I've seen the metamorphosis. He's a beautiful monarch.

A mother can always find the goodness in her child, even if no one else notices. Okay, so it would be better if he would just make a car payment! I'm glad I never really gave up on him, though. But then, I'm the kind of mom who, if he were in jail right now, would think *his* license plates would be *especially* fine.

So if you think you cannot bear one more minute with your sassy teen, hang on. You've only got a little way to go. A few more parties to clean up after, a few more curfews to uphold, one more report card to put up on the refrigerator. There's only a short time left with your little one. They've got only a couple more hysterical phone calls to their best friends, a few more swear words to slip out, a couple more rollings of the eyes, sneers on the lips, and it's over. That is, unless they have younger siblings.

BAM! The Nineties: It's All Good! Sorta

Every second in this world it is dawning on parents everywhere that they have given birth to a teenager. I knew it was coming; after all, I have several friends who are older than myself and they have survived the ordeal. They don't twitch when they speak or have extreme bouts of

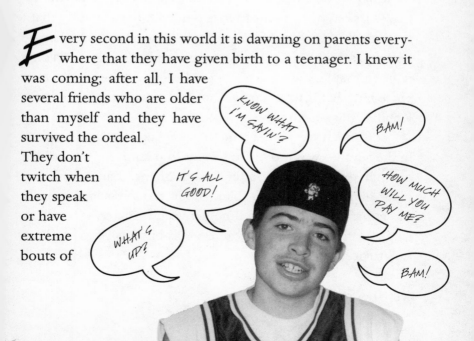

KNOW WHAT I'M SAYIN'?

BAM!

IT'S ALL GOOD!

HOW MUCH WILL YOU PAY ME?

WHAT'S UP?

BAM!

depression. They lived to tell about it and so I figure I will, too. The amazing thing is that the moment you recognize a change in that sweet little boy you realize it was a change brought on by the words of an optimistic parent who never really believed that the "hormonal hurricane" would hit their calm little nucleus. The words are those that you speak for the first time when another parent of a teenager says, "Wow, is our thirteen-year-old turning the house upside down!" I felt my response to that come out of my mouth like a rushing stream that I couldn't take back: "Really, you know, we haven't noticed a change in our son yet."

That was the exact moment when lightning hit! Doors slammed, and in general the only words to leave his mouth have become short monosyllabic grunts or intermittent bursts of air that display his feelings of intense irritation when I do something as simple as requesting that he replace the lid on the mayonnaise jar. I had no idea that ptomaine was so hip.

It helps that I had my children at twenty-two and twenty-five years old because his friends remind him constantly that I am actually pretty cool for a parent. I know he cringes when he hears that, but deep down I know he thinks I'm okay. His only regret is that I'm not on a hit show like *Friends*. I've tried to convince him that it would only ruin the fantasy he has going for Jennifer Aniston anyway.

At thirteen years old, I remember feeling as if I had no place in the family. I was too old to be cute and innocent, yet not old enough to go bowling after Thanksgiving dinner with my older siblings. When you think about it, adolescence is really the gutter of life. It's that time between being old enough to laugh at the dirty joke your uncle tells but too young to have experienced its dirtiness.

My son Bryce certainly seems to be the norm, and I'm guessing that even the most normal teenager in any house can bring turmoil. If only there was a handbook I could follow . . . you know, rules, such as: When dropping off on the first day of school walk at least twenty feet behind your teenager, until further signaled to hand over the money for the books that he swore he wouldn't need for another two weeks. I should have realized that this hurricane was coming.

Think about it, every single child expert from Penelope Leach to Dr. Brazelton ends their books at age twelve. Now I know why. From minute to minute those chapters would not apply. One minute the conflicted child is hanging on your neck and trying to return to the womb, the next minute he is imitating gang members with his hunched-over walk and waving hand signs in the air. I guess that's the new meaning of hip.

They are a breed among themselves. I thought that at this point in our lives it would be me who would be a real embarrassment to my teenager; instead it is turning out to be quite the opposite. The truth is, he is starting to say and do things that are making me cringe. I feel sorry for any oldest child because he has no one older to help guide him through this awkward time. I had lots of older siblings making sure that I didn't make the mistake of publicly professing my love for Donny and Marie. They taught me that "cool" was Credence Clearwater Revival and Three Dog Night. They showed me the difference between the grooviness of a "Hang Ten" logo and the dorkiness of a "smiley face." I watch my son kind of flounder in the world of backward hats and sleeveless T-shirts, between The Notorious B.I.G. and Weird Al Yankovic. I wonder where he gets a sense of himself and whether or not I should try to help him, but my husband and I just recently started buying CDs ourselves and we are only up to replacing

the Doobie Brothers. Not to mention that we are about as fa
from the rap culture as you can get. There are times when
totally understand the outfits that come through the door. I se
it all around me, so he can't be that far off where fashion is con
cerned. Now, the phrases he uses are a whole other story. On
of his favorites is the word "BAM," but it is the word "BAM
said loud, sharp and with a slightly southern twang. "BAM
means that something is good, or I'm proud of myself. Fo
example, "Honey, how'd you do on the math test?" He tosses i
at me and yells, "BAM!" That means he got an A. It's so silly i
makes me giggle to the point of embarrassment for him. I'd
almost prefer a C without a "BAM!" I can't help wondering if
everyone is saying BAM or if this is an identity thing of his
own. I haven't heard any of his friends use the word, nor have
I seen it on ESPN or *The Real World,* the teenage handbook on
MTV.

It's hard to have a conversation with him because it
seems as though I need a courtroom defense for everything that comes out of my mouth. Nothing is light and breezy
anymore. A casual reference to the weather can bring an
onslaught of opinions on "Why do adults care so much about
the weather?" and "Who cares what the temperature is?" and
"It's not gonna change what you're doin' today anyway, so why
does it matter?" and on and on and on, until you just are
silenced out of desperation. We often tiptoe around the house,
careful not to say anything that may awaken the sleeping
teenager. I hear parents complain all the time about how late
their kids sleep. I like it. In fact, teens who sleep until one or
two in the afternoon are actually being protected from themselves, and the fewer hours we all spend together, the better.

The one thing that's great about having that teenager in the
house is that when they finally do wake up they have this great

energy around them. There is always action in the house. Lots of coming and going, the phone ringing . . . I love that. Most of the time. The only time when it is not good is when that energy involves the police or the Internet. Marilyn told me it would happen, but I didn't listen to her. I said those evil words of self-betrayal, "That will never happen to me!" and the next thing I know, "BAM."

My kids had been bugging us for months to get our computer "on line." We were hesitant, mostly because my husband and I both believe it is never good to have anything in the house that your kids know more about than you do. Yet, as always, they wore us down until we were numb. The day my husband finally gave in, we were on our way to the Emmys with Marilyn and her husband. We were actually going to be interviewing stars for our talk show as they came down the red carpet. George Clooney was the hot interview to get that year. We felt more like housewives on a mission to look into his eyes than the faux journalists we were pretending to be.

Minutes before leaving for the night, my husband called America Online and gave them our credit card number to get on the Internet. Also at that time you are required to give them your password. Well, my husband was caught a little off-guard and gave them a shortened version of our old hometown and after it some year that was significant to only him. So our password forever would be "Peta92," short for Petaluma and his year of choice. The kids were happy and we were guaranteed an evening of peace. Our thirteen-year-old was baby-sitting and we figured if he was preoccupied with the Internet there would be no blood spilled that night. Okay, so we bribed them—remember, it worked with potty training?! We left in an elegant flurry while our older son began his first foray into a chat room.

At about ten o'clock that evening, somewhere between Brett Butler, who snubbed us, and Julia Louis-Dreyfus, who gushed over us, and just as George Clooney was making his way down the red carpet, I was paged! When the page is from home you go into your parental mode. Never mind that we were at the Emmys. George would have to wait. My husband and I went in search of a phone. So there was my husband looking like a dead ringer for Kurt Russell, in a tux, on a borrowed cell phone at the Emmys. He got to enjoy the feeling for all of about two seconds. "Hi, honey, it's Dad, is everything okay?" There was nothing but tears and hysteria and blubbering on the other end of the line. Our ten-year-old, Eric, finally grabbed the phone from the thirteen-year-old who was supposed to be "in charge" and muttered something about the computer, the Internet and a woman. We had no details, since it was hard to hear over the deafening cheers for the one man I came to see that night, so we decided we had better go home.

I had to leave poor Marilyn behind the "interview hedge" all alone. You've seen that hedge on the news, where all the journalists behind it are leaning forward, ruining their $10,000 dresses and tuxedos, desperate to get two words from George Clooney. We got home only to find that Bryce had gone into a chat room and pretended to be a forty-two-year-old divorced man! That was just the beginning of the problem. It seems as though that description he gave, combined with the wonderfully creative password "Peta92," had the Web world thinking he was also a pedophile. Bryce made some friends that night who made suggestions to him that were less than appropriate for the ears of a thirteen-year-old boy. I begged him to tell me what was said. He was too embarrassed to say it and was frightened by what he read. He would only say that someone with ne password "LOLITA" said some very nasty things. There was no "BAM" coming out of his mouth that night.

As parents, we had made a big mistake. We immediately changed our password. Thankfully, he had given no one our phone number or our address. "LOLITA" and her friends would have to take their computer sleaze elsewhere. I never did meet George, but we all learned big lessons that night. My teenager still needs me, hip or not. Maybe I should rethink the bribery technique, and the next time we go to the Emmys, Marilyn and I won't be talking to George from behind some hedge.

Knickknack,
Paddy Whack,
Buy Yourself
Some More Crap!

Elvis Is Alive and on My Roof

 believe a person's knickknacks say a lot about them. Sure, some of it is only a reflection of the popular trends, but I tend to hang on to the stuff that's really "me." Like rocks. I love rocks. I have bowls of rocks, rocks on silver trays, rocks on my windowsills, big ones on my hearth and little ones lining my bathtub. Rocks. I like the endless variations, the subtle color changes, the smooth texture and how they look when they're wet. Rocks are stable. Rocks weigh a lot.

Now that I have revealed my love of them, I am afraid certain friends and relatives might try to get me rocks to add to my collection. Isn't it great when you find out someone has begun collecting little things? It makes gift giving sooooo simple. Make sure you collect something you *really* like. When you have a "theme" going on, you tend to get presents even when it's no occasion at all. "Oh, I just saw this cute cow and thought of you. I couldn't resist!"

One year Richard wanted me to draw a bigger-than-life-sized Elvis on a huge piece of plywood to put on our roof at Christmastime. He cut it out, we painted it and he worked some blinking lights up and down his pant legs (it was Elvis, the bloated years). From the moment that decoration appeared on our rooftop, we began receiving Elvis paraphernalia for every birthday and holiday thereafter. I've never been to Graceland, but you'd never know it by looking at my Elvis collection. Actually, Elvis bugs me.

Make sure you begin collecting knickknacks most others will appreciate, as well. A cousin of mine had such a large clown collection that my boys refused to go in her house. "Mommy, please don't make us go inside. There are evil clowns in there." I wished they had not seen *Poltergeist*.

You never know where your knickknacks may take you. Their influence may even lead you to a new future. My cousin Dona used to collect owls. In the seventies, she had hundreds of ceramic, plastic and macramé owls all over her house. Now she rescues real ones.

The beauty of knickknacks is in the eye of the beholder. My mother-in-law had one of those pink knitted toilet paper covers in the shape of a poodle sitting right on the sink at eye level if you were sitting on the throne. One Easter afternoon I could ear it no longer. I hid the poodle. When I went to the bathroom only an hour later, as if by magic, there was a new mint green poodle in its place.

My mom has an odd collection of realistic-looking stuffed and ceramic life-sized toy dogs and cats sitting, lying and curled up all over her house. I always get fooled for a second. Last time I visited, she had a pride of lion cubs sitting on my old bed among two of her beautiful old fur stoles. I wasn't sure if the fur represented the lair, a nest or the kill.

One year I was collecting unusual picture frames and Caryl decided she needed to collect something, too. She mentioned that she saw the bonus of getting gifts for no particular reason. She had the worst time trying to settle on something. We'd go into stores and she'd pine for a collectible. She knew it had to be something she really liked or she'd have to live with multiple irritating items for a long time. She considered and rejected angels, ducks, ivy, gargoyles, salt and pepper shakers, fine jewelry and hats. She never did find anything. Her favorite things in her house are lovely, rich-looking and stylish, but you might call her knickknack-barren.

I have gone through many knickknack phases. Each of my husbands had no choice but to tolerate them. When I was in high school, it was frogs and anything Beatle-like. Later it was black-and-white posters of movie stars from the twenties, homemade candles with psychedelic stripes and artwork from my fellow classmates. I went through a kitsch stage of mammy cookie jars, hula dancers and Felix the Cat wall clocks. I've framed Marcy's letters to the tooth fairy, a piece of her "blankie" and love notes from each kid. I've got leaves from my favorite tree, crystals, crude pottery, antique candleholders, lamps, tassels and my favorite: irons. Yes, the kind you press

your clothes with. My mother used to iron; I prefer to decorat
with them.

Actually, if you were to look around my house right nov
you would see a little bit of each one of my phases filling up
every possible space. There are those who call it eclectic, oth
ers call it a mess.

Beanie Beanie Beanie Can't You See . . .

Sometimes the Beans Just Hypnotize Me

*F*rom time to time there is a collecting trend that grabs everyone around the neck and sucks us in. To some it may be an insane quest for a trivial toy, but in it lies the very heart and soul of parenting, making our children happy! In the past, it was Cabbage Patch dolls, Ninja Turtles and Power Rangers. There always seems to be a shortage of specific ones.

The one you don't have and can't find. If you were there, you know what a bitch it was to find Michelangelo Turtle. Then it was the *white* "Power Ranger" that was the coveted one. Then there was Tickle Me Elmo. On the five o'clock news, we witnessed mothers ripping each other's hair out for the last one on the shelf. Parents were risking prison just to see Johnny smile.

This year the hot items were Beanie Babies, made by a company called Ty. They are little stuffed animals filled with little Styrofoam beans. I had never heard of them until one day my son came home in tears saying that he was the only one in his class who didn't have a Beanie Baby and that some kids had as many as twenty Beanie Babies. "Twenty! Are you crazy, one oughta do it, don't you think?"

"Which animal do you like the most?" I asked.

"I want the Jerry Garcia tie-dyed bear, but it's retired," he said.

"Retired! Honey, Jerry Garcia is dead."

"No, Mom, they don't make that one anymore, but that's the one I want. I can get it at the toy store, they keep those ones in a special cabinet."

I said, "Fine, Mommy will get you the Jerry Garcia bear." I felt the competitive side of me well up. "Mommy's gonna get you that special bear," I said with confidence. No child of mine would be left out of a trend. Besides, these things were only six dollars apiece, it wasn't like it was going to break me.

So we planned a special trip, just Eric and I, to the Beanie Baby store. By the way, whatever the trend is, that becomes the name of the store, never mind that they carry another twenty thousand items. We got there and it was as if Eric were an employee. He went straight to the secret cabinet in the back and asked for the Jerry Garcia bear. The clerk pulled it down as Eric's face lit up the storeroom. "Thank you, Mommy, thank you!"

Inside I was thinking, "Boy, aren't those other kids stupid. This was so easy, all you had to do was ask. What is the big deal?"

We got up to the cashier and I pulled a twenty-dollar bill from my purse. The checker looked at me and said, "That's one hundred and twenty dollars, ma'am."

"What, are you crazy? These things are six dollars." Eric began to cringe, sinking lower and lower behind the counter. "Mommy, he's retired, remember?"

"No kidding he's retired . . . we'd all be retired if we were selling fifty cents' worth of Styrofoam for one hundred and twenty dollars."

Jerry would have to go back to the "special cabinet." Eric had to settle for Sly the fox, which was there in abundance. At that moment I knew this was a trend like no other.

As the weeks passed, the energy behind Beanie mania began to swell. I had a girlfriend who was so sucked in on a personal level that she was driving to LAX in the middle of the night because the gift shops at the airports were getting the first shipments of Beanie Babies. While there on her runs, Glenda befriended the flight attendants. With them, she began a Beanie delivery network so complex, it was only to be rivaled by FedEx. If Glenda could get the flight attendants on American to get the bulls named Snort from Chicago, then she would deliver them in exchange for the leopards named Freckles to the Northwest flight attendants who had brought in the frogs named Legs from Minneapolis. This girl had it down. All the kids in the class wanted to be adopted by Glenda. She was always so generously doling out her extra Beanies to all the kids at no charge.

In the beginning it was fun and innocent, but soon it turned ugly. It became like the Beanie Cartel. Beanie Babies became so hard to get that Beanie information became guarded. People were refusing to disclose their Beanie sources, even to Glenda. That was heresy. Your social ranking at school became based on how many Beanies you had at home. It had become a Beanie world gone mad. Then we started reading in the news about how the Beanie delivery trucks were being heisted at gunpoint. I always checked to see if Glenda was involved and if I needed to bail her out. After all, she did give my son more than thirty Beanies. I felt I owed her.

Then, as soon as the Beanies blew in, it all stopped dead. Eric came home and said, "Mommy, everybody in the class has a Tamagotchi but me."

I said, "A what? A Kristi Yamaguchi?"

"No, it's a digital baby. It's a key chain with a make-believe baby inside and you have to take care of it or it dies."

"Great, and what are we going to do with all the Beanie Babies?"

That very Saturday we called every Target store in the L.A. area in search of Tamagotchis. They were all sold out except for one store that said they had plenty.

We jumped in the car like the Cartwrights out on the range and headed for Target. They had a limit of one per customer, so myself, Eric's grandma Eleanor and Eric walked into Target careful not to look as if we knew one another. We had strict instructions to follow Eric's lead. We quickly discovered, after twenty minutes of walking around like we were playing *The Man From U.N.C.L.E.*, that they had sold out, too. This was getting ridiculous. Once again my underprivileged child had to settle for the knockoff version, a Nano Baby. He knew not to press me after the Jerry Garcia debacle.

Well, Nano proved to be a real drag-o. These little key chains had alarms on them and every time it rang this cyber-

aby had to be attended to. When it had digital droppings, you had to change its diaper; when it got tired, you had to put it down for a nap. When Eric had things to do he left me in charge of cyberbaby. Needless to say, I really had no patience for this trend. Whoever invented this thing had to be childless. They thought it would be fun and teach kids responsibility, I suppose.

The first hour in my care, Nano Baby bit the big one. "That's it," I declared, "no more trendy toys. You have a ton of toys in your closet. The first thing we are going to do is sort out all the stuff you don't even play with anymore and give it away."

I marched that boy into his room, flung open the closet door and a thousand Pogs came tumbling down on top of us.

Do's and Don'ts

I have a hair issue. I think a lot of women do, too. I have thin hair and it's only been about a year now that I've had just enough therapy to experience some mild appreciation for my fine follicles.

I used to overcompensate for my weak hair by having someone else's hair glued onto mine. I never knew whose tresses I bought, but I did know it came from Italy. The process took five hours every five weeks. I would come home thrilled that I, too, had a massive ponytail that swung to and fro with grace, instead of my own puny collection of auburn spiderwebs try-g to pass for hair. I'd give thanks at night to Gina, or Albina, Lena, or even Mario, for that matter.

What is it about our hair that speaks so loudly? It can make break a mood, I tell ya. I'm fascinated by the pioneer women who journeyed the trails west. Forget about the hardships of travel, forget about the loss of possessions, forget about having babies alongside the road. What I can't fathom is all those months of enduring dirty hair.

Before I discovered adding more hair to my few, I used to have a little photographic trick. Whenever I got my picture taken, I would quickly sweep all my hair to the front, then, if the photographer walked toward my backside, I'd whoosh it all back. Can you imagine being that aware of your hair? I bet my fellow thin-haired friends know just what I'm talking about.

I used to covet others' hair. One time I was in a department store when I saw the most exquisite ponytail on a ten-year-old girl. I came up to her and told her how beautiful her tail was. When I began to caress it, her mother appeared from nowhere and whisked her away from me. I yelled out to them, "Is it for sale?" Without looking back at me, she pulled the girl closer to her and quickly disappeared.

I'm much better now. Marcy is particularly thankful for that. When she was in the third grade, still thinking of that little girl, I bought Marcy the cutest bit of a ponytail made in Italy for her hair. She was not at all interested in adding on, but one day I got her to wear her hair in a ponytail with the little Italian piece clipped in. I convinced her that no one could ever tell that she was wearing a piece. It looked *very* cute that way. When she got home, I found the piece in her backpack. Concerned, I asked her what had happened. She barked, "Mom! I was so embarrassed! It was lice check day!"

Three years have passed since that dark day. I no long-
covet. I actually love Marcy's hair just the way it is naturally an
I even like my own short hair without any add-ons. Like I sai
I've had the correct amount of therapy. Maybe some day I'll l
the real color loose.

Having spiderwebs for hair isn't the only thing that will
give you a hair issue. In fact, I have really good hair and
it's one of my best assets, but having good basics doesn't guar-
antee that you always love what God has given you. I get bored
with my hair's straightness. Every now and then a new hairdo
will catch my eye and I have to have it. You can bet that if a new
hair trend pops up, most of us are at least going to think about
trying it. Never mind that it might not work on each of us,
that's always a secondary concern. The perm has become my
own personal symbol of making that very mistake.

I was in a deep hair rut one year and everyone around me
was curly. I wanted curly. I needed a fresh hair pick-me-up. It
was the year *Yentl* came out. I thought Amy Irving was so cute,
I wanted her hair. Unfortunately, I was starting with stick-
straight hair and bangs that I had been impatiently growing
out. Well, those bangs, all curled up, became this huge wad of
fuzz that sat askew on my forehead. When friends who hadn't
seen the new hairdo approached me, their heads automatically
tilted to the side of my wad as they greeted me. They'd say,

Oh, you got a perm . . ." We all know that a statement without a compliment is a dis. The real tragedy occurred when the perm began to grow out. I looked like a Jerry Springer guest. I have sworn never to do it again. Just to keep me an honest woman, I display myself with the wad in a photo on a table in my living room that I am forced to pass every day. It was so wrong!

I have an entire closet full of "following the group" reminders. I have ten pairs of pointy pumps, and a cotton Forenza sweater from The Limited in every color. I have Ditto jeans and Candies from the eighties. I have prairie blouses and dresses made of Qiana. I'm afraid to throw it away—it's always good for a laugh and a costume. I know it will be back, it's just a matter of time. I wonder if someday what I'm wearing now will be worn to some "Let's dress like the nineties" party.

If I had to describe fashion now, I would have to say that my friends and I are all starting to dress like our furniture. I have vests made out of the exact slipcover fabric on my couches. I

have both a summer dress and a chair made out of that tropi-
cal forties fabric that is so popular. What does that say abou
us? I think we have lived in the burbs far too long.

We are all so guilty of consuming. My group of friends alone
is personally responsible for holding up the entire economy in
the state of California. Often I'll look at a credit card bill and I'll
see an entry for something like Macy's-Activewear-$125.
Activewear? I'm hardly active and I can't even tell you what it
was I bought. I'll look around my home and think, "I don't
even like that vase that I had to have a month ago." Our never-
ending quest for stuff has even transferred over to our children.
They live in a world of "I've got to have it!" Sometimes it's the
newest Nike high-tops at $140 a pair. They are sure these shoes
will make them play better. Recently they've been begging for
Nintendo 64, the video game system that has much better
graphics than the three they have in the closet. I refuse,
but I understand. The excessiveness is starting to eat away
at me.

I'm starting to see myself in my children. Consuming
makes me feel so many things. Mostly good things. I reward
myself for how hard I work when I get something new. I feel
happy and superior in a new pair of black shoes, especially if
Marilyn doesn't own them yet. I'm a better cook with a new
kitchen gadget and I write a beautiful check with a brand-new
pen. Unfortunately, it's only for a moment. It's like a runaway
train. I'm so conditioned and ready to buy that I keep buying
the same things over and over again. How many white T-shirts
from the Gap do I need to make me happy? How many pillows
on the bed? How many candles?

Usually one side of the family is more of a spender than the
other. I'm the guilty party. I admire my husband's restraint and

bility to go with so little. Unfortunately, I also admire the new summer clothing line.

I don't worry too much about the problem because compared to others, I know I have a very mild case of it. One summer my sister Marilyn (yes, I really have a sister named Marilyn, too) was at home with her three daughters and pregnant with another. She was due to deliver the next day. She was waiting for labor to set in while watching the shopping channel. She showed me how consumerism can really take control of a rational woman's mind. She had become fixated on the Snackmaster infomercial. The Snackmaster is simply a fancy name for a fancy waffle iron. It has different-shaped sides that allow you to turn white bread into everything from faux apple fritters to grilled cheese sandwiches. Marilyn, the poor thing, was hot, pregnant and overdue. She got sucked in and decided this simple appliance would be the key to making her summer stress-free. She dialed the number to order one and got a busy signal. She began to panic. She tried for an hour straight as she watched the pitchman count down how many Snackmasters were being sold every minute. She became frantic, fearing that she would be the only housewife in America without the Snackmaster! She called me from 500 miles away to see if I could get through to the Snackmaster. No luck. She called our brother in North Carolina to see if he could get through to the Snackmaster. No luck again. She was sweating and pacing as the number of available Snackmasters began to dwindle from 500 to 420.

I said, "Marilyn, get ahold of yourself. Calm down, you can make a grilled cheese sandwich in any pan."

She said, "You don't understand. If I don't have that appliance, nothing can turn white bread into apple turnovers like the Snackmaster. The Snackmaster is the only thing that can right here and right now, change my life for the better."

Granted, that's a lot of pressure to put on an appliance, but in that statement lies the very reason we need more stuff. It makes us feel good and symbolizes the control we all long for.

She went into labor before ever getting the Snackmaster, but after all night on the phone, I got one and brought it to her in the hospital with some pink booties and a loaf of white bread.

I think more men than woman don't understand the obsession. I told my husband, "Look, it could be worse, at least I don't drink." He said, "Honey . . . drinking would be cheaper."

Where Does That
Leave us?

Who's Embarrassing Whom?

embarrass (em bar' es), *v.t.* To make uncomfortably self-conscious; cause confusion and shame to; disconcert, abash.

*W*e go about our business trying to impress others that we are intelligent, capable, creative human beings. We also know that to err is also to be human and, lucky for us, in today's casual atmosphere we can usually laugh at our mistakes. I make so many that people around me feel real good about themselves. It takes a lot to embarrass me, though. I do stuff most people shudder at. The more I let it out, the more I let it go. Not everyone can be that cavalier. Remember poor Dan Quayle? He probably didn't sleep too well the night he added that *e* to "potato." Everybody jumped all over him. I was just grateful it wasn't me, because when I first heard about it, had to ask someone, "What did he do wrong?"

When Aaron was three he loved to watch a popular TV show called *Emergency!* His father was a firefighter and Aaron loved to visit the firehouse to see the trucks and emergency equipment. For about four months he insisted that I tie an oscillating lawn sprinkler to his back. He thought the lawn equipment looked like the tanks firefighters and paramedics wore. I was wishing the clerk and customers at the grocery store had his imagination, then I wouldn't have to walk behind him explaining to all those raised eyebrows that he just wanted to look like Randolph Mantooth on *Emergency!*

I wouldn't call that embarrassing. That wasn't so bad. Sure, going along with Webster, I was a little uncomfortable. A little self-conscious. After all, how many kids do you know who go shopping with a sprinkler on their back? I was *much* more uncomfortable when my daughter was that age and she would wear nothing but the same cheap pink frilly party dress day after day. However, I always had my handy "Oh, she's such a big girl . . . she dresses herself now" disclaimer to eliminate the embarrassment.

When Aaron was fifteen and entering his manly-man stage, he came close to embarrassing me when he began hunting. The act of hunting defenseless creatures is embarrassing enough, but that's only the setup to the real story. It was only after his maiden hunt that he was sensitive and became upset when he shot that first bird, but he got over it quickly. Soon he downed another, then another. You can imagine how very proud I, The Daughter of All That Is Loving and Natural, was about having a rifle-carrying Jethro for a son. While other mothers bragged of how their sons had joined the ski club or the band, mine got together with other little hunters and their osse fathers to kill defenseless creatures of the woods, all in e name of the holy waters of young manhood, Lake estosterone. When the boasting moms asked me about aron, I would simply tell them about my other children. Still, was only really embarrassed when my judgmental vegetarian iends rolled their eyes and asked if he was bothering the spotted owl.

One very special evening, Richard and I were having about twelve people over for a celebration of our tenth wedding anniversary. The dinner was in honor of those people in our life who we perceived had an important influence on our lasting relationship: our therapist, our sister-in-law, a neighbor. You know, those whose shoulders we leaned on and whose phone was overused when we had a problem, some of whom, I might add, were friends of the spotted owl. We had worked for days on the food preparation. We gave each person a significant gift in thanks for their support. Everything was thought out and had to be just right.

Before our guests arrived, Aaron must have come in through the garage and slipped upstairs to his room. His experience in the woods slinking behind trees and bushes paid off, because I didn't even know he was home. Richard and I were serving cocktails and hors d'oeuvres. As I looked over toward our friends sitting in the living room along the window seat, something caught my eye. Had a large bird just flown too close to the window? I saw it again, and our friends also caught a slight glimpse, causing them to snap their heads toward the moving object. No one could quite make out what the heck it was. Some creature seemed to be flying vertically right near the front window.

Aaron's bedroom was directly above the front room. In a moment of mischief, he had proudly strung a lifeless squirrel carcass on the end of a fishing hook, leaned out his upstairs window and was causing Dead Rocky to "fly" by my friend. Apparently he had not only triumphantly shot his first furry critter, but he experienced his first taxidermy attempt that day as well. Gross as it was, and it was extremely gross, I'm not without a sense of humor. I giggled at the practical joke, then told him to stop it, *not* to go downstairs and do get rid of that pelt.

The flying squirrel caused a little confusion, but we all laughed it off. Webster pointed out that confusion is one of the elements of being embarrassed. The worst was yet to come.

The moment Richard, myself and our honored guests sat down to dinner, I heard a low, guttural growl. Though I was starving, it was not my stomach. It sounded as if it was coming from under the table. I eyed my husband and gave the silent facial signal, "Do you hear that?" He looked back with the "I don't know what the hell it is" look. Luckily, our guests were all getting along and chatting away. Then I heard it again. It was a horrible, long, low, animal growl. Had the squirrel come back to life? Could we be hearing a vindictive brother squirrel waiting under the table to seek revenge on Jethro? What *was* that noise? I lifted the tablecloth slightly and saw, to my horror, that our cat had found one of the squirrel paws. Aaron, still being new to taxidermy, didn't know how to reattach the paws. The cat had one gripped tightly in his mouth and was acting very territorial under there. I suppose our guests' feet were a threat to him with his cache. We were able to scoot the cat out before anyone caught on about the appetizer he had clamped in his mouth.

Okay, that was *potentially* embarrassing, but we got out of the danger before we were caught. Besides, it would take more than a squirrel's paw to embarrass me.

Teenagers, on the other hand, leave the door wide open. If you really want to embarrass your teen, just be yourself, be with them and be in public. Everything we do just kills them. Caryl's fourteen-year-old forgot his lunch last week and asked if she'd swing by the school and drop it off. He literally meant swing by and drop off because he begged her not to stop. Forgetting his lunch wasn't the embarrassing part. Having his mom toss it out the window as she kept going didn't bother him, either. But God forbid that anyone should see his mother walking kindly toward him with a sack lunch in hand.

My daughter's twelve now and she has me intimidated. This year the school needed a parent volunteer to help out every Wednesday morning. She asked me if I would please take the position. After the arrangements were made, she told me that I *must* follow her rules:

Rule #1: "Don't flap your hands in the air when you get excited." (Do I do that?)

Rule #2: "Don't ever call me any endearing names."

"But . . ."

"But nothing. Call me by my first name only. No mushy nicknames and don't put any special style into how you say it."

She looked very determined as she told me Rule #3 :"Have a clear memory. Don't forget things."

"I . . . I don't know if I can do that. It's too hard."

"Sure you can, Mom. Oh, one more thing: Don't disco."

Disco? When have I ever discoed? I was busy chasing two little kids during that era. I was doing the Hassle while Travolta and the Kotter kids were doing the Hustle.

I was a wreck getting ready for that first class at my daughter's school. What to wear? What to wear? Nothing too youthful, nothing too dorky. Was my hair too puffy? My makeup too dark? Will I inadvertently disco? I was trying way too hard.

That girl of mine was serious. It was impossible not to embarrass her. She should count her lucky stars. Her older brother could tell her horror stories about the things we used to do to them.

It was so much fun to embarrass the boys. Once in a while they were good sports about it, even. We did little things like sing "Footloose" in public or drive them around in the back of our old wagon with a rubber chicken hanging out the side window. Richard loved to draw attention to them by honking at cute girls and telling them that we have some goooooood-looking dudes hiding in the backseat. Now, I realize what we did to those young, vulnerable adolescents is a form of torture and we should confess it to a therapist, but it was quite an invigorating release! Aaron wasn't the only predator.

Sometimes the boys would bring on their own demise. During the teen years, I was on this kick where I wanted to know that my teenage son understood exactly how much I loved him. Our conversations had diluted down to a series of questions from me answered by a series of grunts from him. I could no longer pull him on my lap and kiss him all over, tickle him and tell him how special he was to me. His life had become a swirl of girlfriends, school friends and squirrel friends. He was gone so much, I could hardly catch a moment. I would try to show him how much I loved him in my own special ways, like fixing his favorite meal or buying him a new earring, but did he really know it? I thought Paul Simon's mother was the luckiest woman in the world because she knew without a doubt that young Paul not only understood that his "Mama loved him like a rock," but sang it to the whole world. So I began to bribe Aaron.

Anytime he wanted something from me like a ride to a friend's or money for a movie, I would say, "Only if you sing it to me," and he would be forced to sing through clenched teeth, "My mama loves me."

"Again, please," I would encourage.

"My mama LOVES me," teeth still clenched.

"How does she love you? I mean, compared to what?"

"She loves me like a ROCK!"

"Yes, she does! Okay, now we can go." And I would take him to his destination knowing he heard it. Thank you, Paul Simon.

I was in the mall one afternoon with Aaron and his friend Jason. Well, we weren't exactly together—that rarely happened during that era—but we did arrive together. I was busy deciding between a new sweatsuit and a really cute sweater. The sweater was winning out when he came upon me in line and asked if I would buy him another pair of $150 Nike tennis shoes. I said no. He began the pleading. I said no. He then looked around at the salesclerk, the women in line behind me, Jason and then, in a low, but very audible tone, started singing, "My mama loves me, she loves me, she gets down on her knees and hugs me. . . . SHE LOVES ME LIKE A ROCK!"

Everyone was silent. Some were staring in confusion, others felt the need to avert their eyes. Jason, in shock and disgust, yelled, "DUDE! What are you doing?"

I said, "You can sing it to the mall, honey, but you're still not getting those shoes." I'm not sure who was more embarrassed, Aaron or Jason.

Sometimes it's nothing more than a common, simple accident that will embarrass us. You know, those dumb accidents you wished no one had seen? I love to remind my neighbor Joanne about the time when some frozen food got the best of her. She was in her garage one morning looking inside her tall freezer for something to defrost when a frozen entree slipped out and fell to the ground. As she bent down to retrieve it, an eight-pound frozen pot roast flew from its position on the top shelf and viciously knocked poor Joanne out cold. Her children got scared and called 911. I remember when the ambulance whirled into the cul-de-sac. We were so worried about her. We didn't know what to think, seeing frozen food strewn all over her garage. Moments later, dazed and completely embarrassed, she woke up in the emergency room, where she was told she had a concussion. The ER nurse, trying to comfort a pink-faced Joanne, told her that she, too, had been accosted by her freezer and had received a broken foot from a nasty frozen chicken.

When Joanne came back home she tried to embellish the story a little to protect her ego, but we just couldn't stop laughing at her. We still do. She got her revenge, though. She got the last laugh, all right. That night she cooked that ferocious roast, she cooked it real good. She said it was the most tender piece of meat she's ever had.

I wonder if Richard would say that Webster's definition is a little too mild for the feelings he experienced that day he was asked to take his boss's paycheck from one office to another. At that time he was low on the totem pole and new to the corporation, which might explain his inquisitiveness about how much money a West Coast executive might pull in. Maybe he was about to set a goal for himself and needed to know if it was really worth the effort. In any case, he was stopped in heavy traffic when his curiosity tempted him to hold that envelope up to the sunlight coming through the front windshield. When the sunshine yielded nothing, he shook it, twisted it, tried to carefully lift up the little window, slightly mutilating it, but still, no income was exposed.

While attempting to use the windshield again, he got an

uncomfortable, self-conscious feeling. Webster? He turned his head guiltily to the right and saw his boss in the car next to him staring right at him. He gave his boss a peevish little wave. Once they both got to the office, his boss's secretary called out, "Hey, Richard. Did Gloria happen to give you Mr. Stinger's paycheck, by any chance?" Richard sheepishly pulled out the envelope from his coat pocket and handed it to his boss, who studied the newly formed creases in it before slipping it into his jacket. No one ever said a word, but Richard still cringes at the memory.

I told you it takes a lot to embarrass me. When the time comes and I do embarrass myself, I get teased and tortured for years by my family. They're still hanging on to the time when our boys were about ten and eleven and had just finished a wild soccer game. It was the tradition for our team to go out for pizza after the game. What am I saying? It was the tradition for every team in Petaluma to go out for pizza and they were all there that one particular evening.

The four of us came in starving. Do you know that kind of starving where nothing's funny? Headaches and nausea are threatening, your hands start to shake and you have one thing on your mind. Food. In this case, pizza.

The line to order that night was very long, there was no place to sit and we just wanted to leave, but other families were encouraging us to have patience. Just as Richard got in line, the kids and I experienced a bit of luck when a whole family got up to leave. We snagged their table, not waiting for anyone to clear it off. We noticed that this other family had left more than half of their large sausage and pepperoni oozing on the platter. The smell was tormenting us. Richard still had five people in front of him. Now, am I the only mother in the world who would do it? You know what I'm talking about. I had to. I just *had* to. My stomach was in charge. I was relating to Mrs. Donner and before I gave it any more thought, I doled out large slices to the kids and one to myself. I even poured them some Coke. I was in the middle of my second piece when the dad of the family came back for the rest of their pizza. He stood there in astonishment and just stared at us. I sat frozen with a string of cheese dangling from my lip to the pizza, my eyes wide. The boys yelled in unison, "Mom!"

For months after the pizza incident, Richard would torture me whenever we'd walk into a restaurant by warning the other diners as we past them to hold on to their food.

You are not human if you've never experienced embarrassment. I just like it better when it happens to someone else.

*T*hey say a mother's love is unconditional. Well, I believe that's true only as long as your child is not embarrassing you. There have been times when our children have said or done something that made us want to duck and hide. There have also been times when moving seemed like the only option to help us save face. It's the old "out of the mouths of babes" thing, but at what age are they no longer considered babes? Is eleven too old?

At our family reunion last summer my oldest brother had come with his new fiancée and her two children. We were happy to see him happy again and were enjoying getting to know Mira and her children. She had spent more than four hours with our family and hadn't run away terrified. There was hope. Mira is from Mexico, a fact only pertinent for you to understand my humiliation.

All forty-five members of my immediate family had piled into the living room to watch a slide show in honor of our brother turning fifty. As usual, there was a technical difficulty. While we were waiting I, thinking myself creative, suggested that the kids all tell their best jokes. There was your typical round of knock-knock jokes and your stupid frog-in-the-blender–variety jokes.

Then my son stood up and said, "I have a joke."

"Okay, honey, tell your joke."

"What do you call four Mexicans in a Ford Fiesta? An American enchilada!"

I wanted to die. My face felt hot and red. I covered his mouth and dragged him from the room. My entire family booed him. They wanted to show their support of Mira and their eagerness to separate themselves from that mentality. Mira gave me a wave from across the room, as if to say, "Don't worry, it's no big deal." She must have seen the steam coming out of my head. My brother, your typical oldest child, was distracted by the pending slide show on his life and seemed to have missed the whole thing.

So much raced through my mind in that one second: "Where did he learn that? . . . Len and I don't condone or use that kind of humor . . . What does everyone think of us? . . . What does Mira think of us?" I felt so humiliated and sorry for my son, who said it with innocence and ignorance. I'm certain of his good values and I was sorry for his poor judgment. I'm also sorry that Mira and her children have to live with that kind of prejudice with regularity. It became a lesson for all of us.

Sometimes humiliation on that level can be a great catalyst for change. That said, I still wanted to put him up for sale.

I wanted Mira and her kids to know that this was the same boy who came home from first grade anxious to tell me about his new friend. A friend whom he really liked. His name was Jose and he didn't speak any English, so they had a hard time communicating. Though Eric was frustrated, I encouraged him to keep trying and assured him that two little boys who want to be friends will eventually be able to understand each other.

Eric went to school the next day, came home and jumped off the school bus bursting with enthusiasm. He said, "Mommy, Mommy, I talked to Jose today!"

I said, "That's great, honey. What did you say?"

Eric said, "I asked him where he was from and you know where he's from, Mommy?"

"No, honey, where?" I asked.

"Mommy, he's from No Comprendo!"

Thankfully, Mira is a very gracious woman. She brushed it off and told me she wasn't offended and never made me feel like a big idiot. I couldn't help wondering if her kids had ever embarrassed her as badly. I just got an invitation to their wedding and we're all on the list. *Gracias por entender, Mira.*

There is one other time that stings as much as that one. This one involves our other son. They all test the waters at least once. My mother- and father-in-law were visiting when our very blunt son asked them if when they die, would we get their money?

Oh my God! They were speechless. I was furious! It sounded as though we all just sit around talking about the day we can go in with labeling guns and start marking our territory. I can assure you we hadn't, but would they believe that? If I were them, would I believe that? These are things that drive families apart. The flippant little comments of kids who obviously haven't been thrown the "don't you even think about it" look often enough.

Now, on occasion I act before anything can possibly go wrong. They simply open their mouth with a questionable tone and I can raise one eyebrow faster than a gunslinger. It is when I'm not around to censor them that I worry. I just pray that some other parent has bought into that "the world is a village" thing and will help out in my absence. So if you happen to be somewhere and you see one of my kids with a foot in his mouth . . . have at him!

Our children aren't the only ones who embarrass us. As long as I can remember, I have been embarrassed at the things my parents did. At thirty-seven, of course, the rate at which they embarrass me is far less than when I was sixteen. As a comedian, at least I can put these moments to good use. I can honestly say that my mother, Saint Claire, as we like to call her, is a never-ending source of material for me.

In the early eighties my mom and some other family members went on the game show *Family Feud*. Saint Claire was the leader, naturally. She was nervous and not sure that she wanted to get all kissy with Richard Dawson. When the bonus round came near the end of the show, the other family won the option and passed it to my family to play. The question was, "What does a girl do to flirt?"

In order to play for the big money, Saint Claire's team only had to get one answer correct. The tension mounted. I, my grandmother and the rest of my siblings sat perspiring in the audience.

We heard my sister-in-law saying over and over, "Giggle . . . a woman would giggle."

Yes . . . that had to be the answer!

Saint Claire made her way to the podium as Richard Dawson grabbed her by the hand. She said, "Richard, we're going to say . . . to flirt a girl would . . . drop a hankie."

"What! Drop a hankie? Maybe in 1940, but not now!"

The cameras flashed to her disappointed family, moaning in the audience. Little did I know that wouldn't be the last embarrassing moment I would have on television.

I'm sure there are things I do that make my children cringe with embarrassment, so I try to be sensitive. I make an effort not to repeat the obvious things that our parents did, like singing too loud in a church when no one else is singing or using your middle finger as a pointer. I can only hope that my kids will fill me in . . . that way I can always use it as a weapon of bribery. That's power Saint Claire never even knew she had.

In Search of a LARGE!

$\mathcal{S}$hopping is a double-edged sword. I love it so much. In fact, it is one of the few things that make me so happy. If only shopping didn't have a downside, but it does. Here's the problem. When I shop for shoes I'm always in heaven because no matter how large I get, I can always find a pair of shoes that fit. Shoes are also about the only clothing item that don't have those unflattering pleats in the front.

I'm a big-boned baby girl. In fact, if I had been raised in Minnesota I would've made one hell of a speed skater. Bonnie Blair has got nothing on my thighs. I would bet anything that in Minnesota it's easier to find a large than anywhere else. I always feel so at home there with all my other big blond friends.

Searching for a large-size anything has become a humiliating experience for all of us bigg'ns. (That's my pet name for the robust, "Rubenesque" type woman.) We've all heard the research that says that the average-size American woman is five feet four inches tall and weighs 142 pounds. If we are the majority, why is it so darn hard to find a size 12 or 14? Is it because they don't make enough larges or is it because they're all hoping we'll lose weight soon?

If you walk into any store in this country you will find the larges at the bottom of the pile or the back of the rack or just nonexistent. We are then forced to root through the pile like a beaver looking for a log. I usually start huffing and puffing and then the salesperson comes over and says, "Do you need some help?"

"No! I need you to put the larges on the top of the pile!"

Then the salesperson starts to root through to the bottom of the pile, as if you're stupid and have just recently gotten large. They always come up empty-handed and then proceed to yell across the entire store to their supervisor. "Hey, Joanie, do we have any larges left?"

The heads of every little size 2 in the vicinity pop up from their halter tops with a look of arrogance, as if to say, "I ate whatever I wanted for lunch, what'd you have?"

Normally I'm absolutely fine with my size. I know I will never see my high school weight again, and that is really okay. After all, it is just a matter of degrees, like everything else in life. I find that when I go to places like Disneyland where there are lots of people all gathered together, I'm feeling pretty good. Just spend an hour in the line to Space Mountain and watch the extremes of humanity pass you by. You'll feel like Vendela, too. In fact, at almost any county fair you can look like a model compared to what just passed you. French fries are definitely America's favorite food. You can always count on women who are far too large to be wearing a tube top and dolphin shorts. It's proof positive there aren't enough larges to be found. I call that "breaking your contract with America." It's okay to be large and it's also okay to show your largeness appropriately. The rule is this: "Chances are, if you are wearing something that's hurting you . . . it's hurting somebody else."

Most people are weird about weight. It's right up there with money when it comes to big "no-nos" at the dinner table discussion. I wish people would just start to call it what it is. If you're dinky you're dinky, if you're a bigg'n you're a bigg'n. The only thing that irritates me with this whole sizing thing is when people start to get cute with what they call their version of sizing. All the ones like "Pretty and Plump" and "Big Gals" have got to go. In fact, any name that implies Omar has got to go. We don't need separate sections or separate stores, we need bigger sizes. Just don't stop at the larges, keep going, XL, XXL, and so on. Lately in the stores you see things tagged with a "One Size Fits Most." Well, most of us bigg'ns are "most" of the people out there and that size is never large enough. So if it really is one size fits most, it should fit most people, the big majority. We should get smart and threaten to do a "sit-on" instead of a sit-in.

Size is only a problem when it is a problem for you on a personal level. I let go of any hope of looking like someone on *Friends* a long time ago. Any honest bigg'n will tell you that when you gain weight to the point that is unhealthy for your own body, you know it. I know when I go to bed and in the middle of the night I think I'm rolling over on my husband but it's really myself. That is my body letting me know when it is time to let up on the Mint Milanos. This whole body image and diet thing is way out of control. We all know what we need to do to be at our best. You start exercising more, eat a low-fat diet and drink a lot of water. The next thing you know you're smelling like a flower! Unfortunately, that doesn't help our love affair with food.

Do you like burgers? I love a great hamburger. I love a well-done cheeseburger more than a rancher does. If someone took away my burgers I would die. Marilyn gives me a hard time because I know the exact location of every drive-through burger place in America, but who do you think she turns to when she's in Cincinnati with a hankering for a double bacon cheeseburger? After a burger comes my love affair with chocolate. I would sell my soul for a Snickers or a brownie. After every meal I need a little taste of chocolate. I've always said it is better than sex and easier to get. I call it my "chocolate topper."

Food is the last great vice. Nobody drinks or smokes anymore, so now people are turning to food. After all, we have to eat. Okay, so maybe not the quantities we do, but when I do eat it I want to enjoy it and not be subtracting on a calculator or pulling "Deal a Meal" fat cards out of my wallet.

I am really beginning to hate my "no-fat" friends. They read every label and count every fat gram and dip their forks into their dressing. It makes eating so un-fun. They say they've been doing it so long that they don't even like the taste of foods with fat in them anymore. Oh, please, give me any one of those overly aerobicized fat-counters asleep. Then let me dangle a carrot on one side and a warm brownie fresh from the oven on the other and I'll tell you where their bony little hands will go. I don't mean to sound bitter, but most of the people I know who can consistently live like that are making a living doing it. They are trainers and teachers and diet gurus, not moms tempted by the crust of a peanut butter and jelly sandwich on the way to buy the birthday cupcakes at the bakery that makes your favorite croissant. Besides, it's better to have friends who are larger than yourself. That's why Marilyn and I are such good friends. Oh, sure, she has those cute little legs, but she's still in the size 12 to 14 range. Whew!

It has taken me a long time to eat what I want in moderation without beating myself up for it. There have been a lot of moments when I was discouraged and felt as though I would only fit in at Sea World. I have also done the dreaded fen-phen diet. I lost thirty-five pounds and thought I had found the miracle, only to realize I had to choose between death and thin. Damn! I've even considered having it all sucked out, but in the end I was just too chicken to try it. That only left therapy. The therapist's evaluation was that I eat because something's eating me. That there's something deep and dark within me. I had to tell her it was the Nestle's Crunch bar in the bottom of my purse. I ate it on the way home from the appointment.

I think my lowest point came when I was driving in my car one day and heard the radio sports announcer speak so enthusiastically of a local high school linebacker who was recently named an All-American. They gave credit to the fact that he had finally hit the 180-pound mark. Well, I was 180 pounds! My all-time high. Twenty-four-32-hut-hut . . .

Shortly after that, it got worse. When Marilyn and I first got the talk show and we were working on the pilot for the show, what we would wear was of great importance to the network. Everything the stylist brought for me didn't fit or looked horrible on me. The big pink flannel blazer was so . . . hippolike. The rose-patterned leggings looked like hibiscus on me. I was a huge tablecloth in the plaid shirt. If I bent over we could've had a picnic on my back. Then I could hear a big discussion going on outside my dressing room. "I think we should get a stylist who specializes in bigger clothes." "I think we should stick to more fitted things that don't make her look so big." Who were they kidding, I big. How low can you go?

The biggest help to me has always been having the ability to laugh about it, be honest about it and concentrate on my assets. I have damn good hair, especially since I don't perm it anymore. My weight fluctuates all the time, so here's how I found a way to not feel sorry for myself and to keep me from skipping a summer in my bathing suit because I feel so gross and so far from *Baywatch:* All it takes is a little reframing.

The best way to reframe is to go to one of those water parks . . . No, I'm just kidding! Who are your heroes? Who are the people you admire the most, the ones who really made a difference in your life? I bet their size is the last thing that comes to your mind. If you said Elle McPherson, then you are on your own and deserve to be miserable.

One of my heroes is an older woman I met on our talk show. Her name is Ellie. She organized a major relief effort for Jews in Bosnia out of her temple in St. Louis, Missouri. Her commitment to never let anything like the Holocaust happen again was so inspiring to me. As I sat there and interviewed her and watched her face and listened to the warmth in her words, I was struck by her strength, not her figure. What she had accomplished was enormous. Marilyn has always considered Rosa Parks to be her hero, and it's not her physical traits that she applauds, it's the stand she took on the bus that day in Montgomery, Alabama. I don't mean to sound presumptuous, but someday we could all be a hero to someone. When that day comes, I want to be able to sit down with them, celebrate and have a great big well-done cheeseburger.

Who Am I?

*D*o you ever look at your life and wonder, "Who am I?" When I was ten I wanted to be a dancer like Cyd Charisse. The year was 1957, and growing up in a small town, generally there was no mention of little girls having a career. There wasn't much mention of college, either, and except for my cousin Geri, who was a secretary for a while, my family had little expectations when it came to their female members. Mostly it was "the wedding" that was put before our eyes on a regular basis. My mother showed no signs of discontent and neither did June Cleaver, therefore I happily followed my destiny.

Questioning the old ways comes naturally when we're in

ur twenties. Turning on, tuning in and dropping out kind of accelerates that process. Looking deep into my ego one psychedelic evening, I decided I should start over. I felt like a floating, following, lost, insecure puppy. And that was without the mind-expanding drugs. My quest for self-esteem began that night in '68. With the help of meditation, philosophical discussions, Don Juan's teachings, self-hypnosis, tarot predictions, dancing as a cigar, having children, Mark Victor Hansen motivational tapes, another husband, the PTA, dream analysis, working with foreign students, a funny neighbor and lots of therapy, I made it! I had become an assertive woman with her self-esteem goin' on. That is, until the day I received my invitation to my thirty-year high school reunion. The idea of returning to high school, if only for one night, sent me right back to 1964. Bye-bye, Miss I-Got-It-All-Together. Hello, Insecurity.

I think that the kind of person we are today is largely influenced by our experience in high school, don't you? So much of my self-image was both developed and stunted during those four years. It's a hard thing to shake off. Here I was, forty-seven years old, and there I sat with that invitation in my hand and my first thought was, "I just want to be popular." Such a mature goal. What a great reflection of all those years in therapy. Thoughts like "Would I be cute enough? Would there be enough time to become thin enough?" started creeping into my psyche. Right away I started stressing over my weight, my clothes, the bags under my eyes, my hair and my canceled TV show. I began biting my nails, eating more chocolate and sleeping fitfully, and when I thought I saw hair loss, I tore the invitation right up.

In 1965, the popular boys called themselves The Crew. They surfed, had wild parties, taught us the dirty words to "Louie Louie," wore pegged pants with cool madras shirts and always

said *"bitchin'."* Everybody wanted to be in The Crew. Those o[f]
us lucky enough to date The Crew called ourselves Th[e]
Crewettes (ah, how very original). It was a girls' world o[f]
laughing, slumber parties, dancing to "Wipe Out," practica[l]
joking, crank calls to the gym teacher, football rallies, intimate
secrets. We'd set our hair in those big orange juice cans, sit for
hours with one of those hair dryers with the bonnets that puff
up. Remember those? They have a little hose that attaches to a
motor inside a little hatbox. We'd wait and wait for that
Dippity-Do to dry, then rat it all up, smooth it slightly over like
a nice shiny helmet and spray the hell out of it with the king of
all hairsprays . . . Aquanet. We had hair of steel, with a little
bow just above the bangs. To this day I can't abide flat hair. We
were hot stuff.

Well, that's the part people saw. That's how we appeared in
the yearbook. That's the first layer. Now the truth. I
M remember how scared and intimidated I was. Do you
recall when the most important thing in your life was to
be accepted? It was hard work to be popular, and I knew it
could be taken away at any minute. My personal insecurity told
me every day what to wear and whom to like. Insecurity
reminded me every minute that I was not tall enough, cute
enough, smart enough and my hair was not big enough.

I hardly had a mind of my own back in those days. I did
whatever the Crewettes did and I was a sucker for five little
words: "I'll be your best friend."

My friend would ask, "Marilyn, will you call John Martin
and see if he likes me? Tell him that I want to go out with him."

"Come on, Vicki. I hardly know John. It'll look stupid if I
call him."

"I'll be your best friend."

"Okay."

There was the day I drove up to school with a carful of girls. "Marilyn, I dare you to drive the car up onto the campus, down the hall, past the lockers!"

"Are you kidding? We'll get busted! I can't afford to get in trouble again."

"I'll be your best friend."

"Okay . . . Hope the car fits down the hall."

I had no mind of my own. I'm just glad Charles Manson didn't go to our high school.

I would stay on the phone until late every night. Told my mom I was doing homework, but if I really think about it, I was whiling away the hours with a little company until I felt sleepy. I never wanted to be alone.

Would *you* want to be sixteen again? So I trust that you understand why I was not thrilled about going back to my hometown high school thirty years later. Why I had no control over my self-esteem, I'll never know, but I became that lost, pathetic adolescent looking for a zit.

Soon after the invitations came out, I started getting calls from the Crewettes, but no one could convince me that it was worth the stress. As a matter of fact, Caryl and I were on the road doing a show in Cleveland the weekend of the reunion. I was still determined not to go when I got the call from Vicki, Head Crewette. She said that she knew for sure that my old boyfriend, Joey Grey, would be there. My heart skipped a thousand beats. I was silent. Then she said the five words, "I'll be your best friend." "Oh . . . kay." So instead of heading back to L.A., I took a deep breath, got a ticket to San Francisco and drove the fifty miles north to Santa Rosa to see if I was still popular. I was really hating the idea that I would have to arrive alone, late. When I was an adolescent, I don't think I ever entered a room alone.

I had no invitation with me and when Vicki explained where the reunion was, she kept saying, "You know where it is."

"I'm not sure, Vicki, it's been a long time."

"Oh, sure you do! It's that hotel they built in front of the place where we all went to make out."

I vaguely remembered, but to be sure, when I arrived, asked the clerk at the hotel first if there was a reunion taking place inside. Everything checked out, so I dashed into the bathroom for a quick hair, circles under my eyes and makeup assessment, took a deep breath and proceeded to go to my high school reunion.

There's something else you should know about me: I don't remember anybody. I didn't remember anybody in high school and it's only gotten worse. To compensate I act friendly, as if I've definitely met each person, because I usually have and they usually get all pissy if I don't remember. Do you do that?

M I was on my own with all my neuroses in place as I nervously wandered through the unfamiliar crowd of graduates with a glass of chardonnay in my hand and a warm smile on my face. My mind was searching, searching, and nothing was clicking. My personal insecurity was kicking in right on time. I was lost and, as usual, faking it. I kept roaming in search of Vicki, all the while hugging and greeting complete strangers. I walked around with my stomach held in and my chin up, just in case Joey Grey saw me before I saw him. I asked a bunch of size-large screaming women if they knew where Vicki was and they said to try the back of the room. I was not feeling popular. As I got there, thank God I noticed the decorations. There were posters of yearbook photographs of "the good old gang" back in high school hanging up. But these pictures depicted the crowning of a prom queen with Farrah Fawcett hair, with boys in ruffled shirts and blue polyester.

oung girls were wearing prairie dresses! See how shallow I
m? Names and faces mean nothing to me, but show me some
ut-of-place Qiana and I'm all over it. I almost said out loud,
"Excuse me, but where is the white lipstick? The bubble hair-
dos? The Empire-waist dresses? Come on, where is Nancy
Devoto, *head* song leader, for God's sake!" Who were these
people? I was considering calling the Alzheimer's Hotline when
I grabbed a nearby waiter and quickly and quietly asked, "Is
this Montgomery High School, Class of '65?" He grinned and
said, "Honey, this is Cloverdale, Class of '75!"

What an idiot I am! Not only was I at the completely *wrong*
high school reunion, but it took me twenty minutes to figure it
out! All those painful, unmet expectations and I'm at the
wrong damn reunion? The extra makeup, the cute little suit,
the handfuls of Advil and I'm in the wrong place? I was
stunned. Class of '75? These people were ten years my junior!
No wonder I had been thinking, "Hey, I'm not the only one
who's had a little face work done," and I was seeing some
mighty realistic rugs on the men, too.

I started to laugh. I was laughing so hard I was ruining my
eye makeup, but I couldn't stop. At last I gave my wineglass
back to the still chuckling waiter and left my fear of reunions
back at Cloverdale High.

By the time I arrived at my real reunion, my classmates
were well into dinner and awards. I think this reunion started a
little earlier to accommodate the age group. Remember, I was
in high school back when the Beach Boys were still boys. I
could see a table of teachers sitting near the door who had
come back, too. When I walked up to them, I realized that it
was my peers at the table, not thoughtful teachers. Oh, Lord,
this definitely was the Class of '65.

As thirty years go by, it's natural to experience yourself

slowly going through the aging process. Actually, you notice it on your friends before you see it on yourself. It comes in tiny increments, first of shock, then denial, next anti-aging creams, Miss Clairol and finally, for some of us, surgery; never is there true acceptance. You often see the flaw, then deny it. It's a series of see, deny, see, deny, see, deny. Deep down inside you've recorded every wrinkle, but you rarely pull that thought up. It's a bitch to watch yourself decompose.

Now fast-forward thirty years and watch the "boys" who first stirred your budding libido jump from age seventeen to a ripe forty-seven. Well, you just lose your breath for a little moment. Let this image serve as a warning to you: It takes Prozac three months to get into your system. Order early! I think Bette Davis said it best when she said, "Aging ain't for sissies."

M I was able to slip into the event fairly unnoticed just as the Tri Tones, the pride of Montgomery High's chorus teacher, were entertaining their fellow grads by re-creating the Glee Club's shining moment with their rendition of "Chim Chim Cher-ee" a cappella. Vicki had saved me a seat at the Crewette table, but I couldn't talk during the medley, so I took in the atmosphere. I began to relax a little. I felt an old sense of belonging as I heard the familiar old songs, joined my familiar gang. Then I scanned the room and noticed how the Drill Team still sat together, so did the Audio/Visual guys, the Pep Club, the cheerleaders, the sluts.

While they were handing out the first award, "How many classmates have been divorced?" I raised my hand and was thinking about what clothes I had on. I had wanted to capture something that would say young, hip, conservative, free-spirited, stylish, motherhood, spiritually evolved and television all at once, but all I had with me in Cleveland was a pair of jeans and ots of costumes. Perhaps I should have gone with my favorite costume, the tight leopard unitard with the baby attached to my leg, but I ran out and quickly bought a black (slimming, you know) suit with a short skirt (my legs being the only body part I allow myself to show). Just as I was beginning to have clothes remorse, I noticed that some people were dressed as though they were on their way to Vegas. I saw quite a few "Mother of the Bride"s, while others looked as if they had come to make a drug deal. And could somebody please tell me why a nearly fifty-year-old woman would wear a high-fashion hat to a class reunion? I felt the strong need to gossip.

The awards continued, "How many people have more than three grandchildren?" Grandchildren?

I began scanning for Joey Grey. We were both sixteen when that wild, uncontrollable, romantic passion first came my way. On October fifth of our junior year he gave me his class ring. I wrapped a long string of angora wool around it to fit my finger and wore it all the time to show off to everyone that we were "going together." We were inseparable for a year.

Whenever I'd double-date with another Crewette, we would play a little game. It was a point system. You got five points for mild kissing. I got five right away. In order to get ten points, you had to allow the tongue. Got that right away, too. I had my own special style of getting fifteen points: I'd lay my head snugly on Joey Grey's shoulder and pretend that I was sound asleep. Then I'd let him think he was sneaking a feel of my breast. After a while I'd pop up and shout, "How could you?" That was the clue to my fellow Crewette that I just got fifteen points. Twenty was my favorite. Twenty points was dry humping. I liked that. Twenty-five was going all the way. Back in 1965 you did *not* go all the way. No way. Not, of course, unless you were a Catholic girl. Oh, come on, didn't we all

know somebody who had to drop out of school because o
mononucleosis? Right. No, I held out on the big twenty-five.
was even Catholic, too, which made Joey Grey a little crazy.

Our relationship was stormy at times, loving at other times,
with the maturity of sixteen-year-olds. We broke up and went
back together on several occasions before I took off the angora
for the last time and gave him back his ring.

That first love thing really sticks with a girl, doesn't it? Even
now he still shows up in my dreams. I don't exactly know why.
Maybe it's my version of Fabio. I ran into him a few times after
high school at parties and other events and my heart would
jump whenever our eyes met. His are *sooo* blue. And that's
what I was looking for while sitting at that table next to Vicki.
There tends to be a lot of prescription eyewear at a thirty-year
reunion.

M Back in '65, our usual obligatory compliment/greet-
ing was "You look so cuuuuute!" meaning: "Your flip is
nice and high today. (But you can see right through it.)"
Thirty years later the common greeting was "You look
goooood," meaning, "You look a little better than I expected."
It could also mean: "Man, you've really aged and, actually, I'm
delighted." The salutation that most often came my way that
night was "You look much better in person than you do on
TV." At one point, I was sort of rescued by a well-meaning,
slightly tipsy old girlfriend of mine with her overenthusiastic
"Well, I think she looks much better on TV than in person!"
Yeah, that's the way to stick up for your old buddy.

The boys of The Crew were a surprise. Almost all of those
wild, surfin', partying guys are now on various levels of a
twelve-step program. It was sort of a disappointment because
lately I've found my clean and sober friends to be irritating.

The night was filled with laughing, dancing, reminiscing

nd gossiping. I left my old insecurity back at that other eunion. The DJ played lots of Beach Boys, Beatles, Temptations, Herman's Hermits, Jerry and the Pacemakers and Aretha. The later it got, the closer I got to giving up any hope of seeing Joey Grey. I even quit holding my stomach in. I was dancing with Barney Squires, an old friend and recent multimillionaire due to his investment in cigars, while the DJ played "In My Room." Barney was entertaining me with his stories of going to the Playboy Mansion when I caught those deep blue eyes looking at me from across the dance floor. I held my breath. It was *Joey Grey*. And he wasn't gray at all. He was bald.

I must say here that every one of my ex-boyfriends is practically hairless now. I remind my husband of this now and again, lest he has any thoughts of leaving me.

It mattered nothing to me. I still saw Joey as being as handsome as ever. You should see those eyes. We started walking toward each other. The crowd parted for us (everybody knew about me and Joey Grey). We hugged and it was long and warm and he smelled of Aqua Velva. The Righteous Brothers were singing, "You're my love, you're my inspiration. You're all I've got to get me by . . ." I didn't want to let go, but I did. We talked a little about our lifestyles and families. He has a wife and a son. I told him I had two husbands and four kids. Apparently I've been a lot busier. Then he told me what every ex–high school sweetheart longs to hear. He said that every once in a while he has a dream about me. That was all I needed. Just that. We hugged again, this time quickly, and said good-bye. It was perfect.

I know . . . I know, you wanted me to get at least ten points, didn't you? Well, I am of the belief that your ex-boyfriend should remain a fantasy. I say, just let the memory of the high

school boyfriend warm you up in a dream or two and hono
your love for your real soulmate. Besides, who are we kidding
If you live with *anybody* for long enough they'll irritate you.
really don't think an old boyfriend of mine would be any bet
ter at giving me a lengthy phone message from my friends that
my loving husband is now. Just let it rest.

I got caught up on some old friends. The big gossip that
night was about Jan Johnston, who had just left her husband
and kids for another woman. After my Joey Grey hug, it's very
likely that people were gossiping about me, too. Over the years
I've come to think of myself as an entertainer, and I figure if
people want to talk about me behind my back, then in a way,
I'm still entertaining them.

Who am I now? Hell, I don't know. I'm just a person who is
on an adventure. Sometimes the ride takes me to scary places,
sometimes sad places and other times it's so much fun. I've
always got this reunion to remind me that I may be old, but I
don't look like a teacher. Yet. I hadn't exactly lost all my confi-
dence, I just stunned it. My original fears of "fitting in" were
just plain silly because, as it turned out, I ended up "fitting in"
at *two* high schools.

I wonder what it'll be like when I'm eighty. Will I be able to
handle anything? I wonder if I'll still be putting on sunless tan-
ning cream or setting my hair in big rollers. I wonder if I'll be
wise. I hope I still have my sense of humor. And I wonder if
that waiter will still be telling the story about the confused old
lady who wandered around the Cloverdale High School
reunion thinking she knew everybody.

Woman, Oh Woman

*A*s our children need us less and less in a physical sense, we are all at the crossroads. We are beginning to wonder, "Where does that leave us?" What am I going to do when I don't have something to bitch about? It seems that I've been bitching about something for so long. I know my friends are thinking it, too, because we all drank too much and cried about it recently. The kids are all going to be gone soon and then that leaves just me and him. This is the time when you'd better do the "check your marriage test" in *Cosmo*. Pretty soon there won't be any kids to hide behind. Not only will we be alone with our spouses, we will be alone with ourselves. As long as there are kids around, none of us really has to face who *we* are. When you have kids, your path becomes predetermined, and for a lot of us that meant putting things on hold in the name of school activities and basketball and all kinds of family business. When they are gone, who will we be? I'm so afraid I'll wake up one day and have no social calendar. Everything we do, every nonworking moment, revolves around our kids. Our friends are their friends' parents. What will I do when there will be nowhere to scurry off to? I do not want to end up taking yoga and doing pet adoptions just to fill up my life.

I already got a puppy to fill the void as I begin to come to the close of my childbearing years. I know it's not a good sign. Yeah . . . right, I told everyone the puppy was for Eric's birthday, but really it's giving me purpose and maybe even a little avoidance from the real issues bearing down on me. My husband's complaining that he's been trying to wake me up at 6:00 A.M. for years with no luck! The minute we got that puppy I was up and out of bed at six sharp. It's sort of like having a baby, only this one can go into a crate all night. It's great.

We all know those people who have tried everything in an effort to "find themselves." Some did it before the kids left home. Some are waiting, but on the cusp of booking a trip to see the Dalai Lama. I'm desperately hoping that I'll be prepared well in advance of an empty nest. That gives me about seven years to do some deep spiritual searching. Eegh, I hate spiritual searching.

With every stage of our children's growth, I learned something new. I became wiser and more tolerant and gained a different perspective as we crossed each bump in the road. Part of me is looking forward to the last big speed bump, yet I also ead it. I'm afraid that when the time comes, I'll be trying to ll my sons and their girlfriends around the block in the agon. I go into their rooms even now sometimes and pull own little toys from just a couple of years ago and weep at the assing of it all so quickly. I'm going to be a mess. In order to ot be the mother who's a drag to be around, I'm going to have o prepare now. I think the only answer is to grab a bunch of irlfriends in weepy sentimentality and "huddle up."

t's funny how that empty nest threatens to sneak up on you. I've wept over empty rooms twice, only to turn around and find them occupied by their former owners again. I love it when my kids come back to live with me. It doesn't appear too pitiful yet, but if my son becomes a security guard and gets falsely accused of planting a bomb in an Olympic park, I'll know it's time to kick him out.

We never know where this adventure called life will take us. Anything can happen in this cartoon. I was forty-two when Caryl and I put together the first hokey Mommies stage show. Two years later, in the middle of an era when the media are completely youth-oriented, I was forty-four and given my own TV show. Granted, I didn't know what the hell I was doing, but neither does anybody else. If I can do it, you can do it. I'm just along for the ride, and what a ride it is. It actually wasn't my lifelong dream to have a television show. I wanted to change

the world. I guess if you have read this book and you feel a l[i]
tle better about yourself, then I'm still on track.

Y ou see, there is nothing like a good woman friend to hel[p]
you put it all in perspective. In my life, I have been blesse[d]
many times in that department. I began to cherish my friend
ships with women in high school. I went to an all-girls hig[h]
school. It was the kind of school that when you said the name[,]
other people would gag and say, "Oh, don't you hate going
there!" I didn't . . . I loved it. It was then that I began to recognize that only another woman can totally understand what you
are feeling when you are feeling it and why that feeling is making you crazy. It's a woman I call when I need that nod of
recognition, someone to say, "I live it too and you're not crazy
for changing the locks on all the doors."

For every major event in my life, I have been supported and
comforted by women. When I got married, my friends were like
a gaggle of geese at my side, singing "Going to the Chapel"
and suggesting the famous knee-high nylons under the wedding dress. When my son was born, my sister Marilyn held my
hand with every contraction and only lied when necessary to
protect me from the pain. When I moved into the burbs,
Marilyn and Judy and Renée helped me sort it all out and kept
me sane. And when Marilyn and I started performing, those
same women and countless others helped watch our kids so we

ould travel and made dinners for our families, who were eating McDonald's four nights a week when we were away. They made sure my children were picked up from school even when Len tried to help out with the carpool and ended up confusing everyone in it. They set up chairs at the community centers where we performed. They laughed even when we weren't funny. (But I would like to remind them that those very lines are the lines they laugh the most at now.) When I was just beginning to do stand-up comedy, my friends would graciously sit and listen to all the material I would run by them. I'm sure it got to be torturous, but they never once ran away, even if their eyes were saying they wanted to.

As we come to that next phase, I hope my friends are equally prepared to be there for me, 'cause here I come. When I was sixteen I used to write embarrassing, dripping-with-emotion poetry and I feel it starting to well up again. Maybe we should all get some journals and mail them back and forth with special, weepy, sentimental entries for one another.

Marilyn is planning to go back to her hippie roots and a commune. I'm not quite ready to think about my friends aging right before my eyes. At this stage, I'm enjoying being surprised when I see them at more natural intervals and I'm counting on them to help me in that spiritual department, too. The truth is, I'm afraid of what I might discover once I'm out of the spin cycle and do find a way to get the lid up, because for all we know, the answer could just be one more big load of wash to be done!

Join "The Mommies" on Their Website

www.candmshow.com

In *The Motherload,* Marilyn talks about embarrassing moments when her son brought home a dead squirrel and when she got caught eating someone else's pizza, and Caryl describes her horror when her kids asked their grandparents who would get all their stuff when they died. Do you have any embarrassing or funny Mommy Moments you'd like to share? If so, visit "The Mommies" website at www.candmshow.com to post a message or e-mail. They would love to hear from you!